P9-CKZ-599

WELCOME
TO THE
TWENTY-FIRST CENTURY

Books by Pierre Berton

The Royal Family
The Mysterious North
Klondike
Just Add Water and Stir
Adventures of a Columnist
Fast Fast Fast Relief
The Big Sell
The Comfortable Pew
The Cool, Crazy, Committed
    World of the Sixties
The Smug Minority
The National Dream
The Last Spike
Drifting Home
Hollywood's Canada
My Country
The Dionne Years
The Wild Frontier
The Invasion of Canada
Flames Across the Border
Why We Act Like Canadians
The Promised Land
Vimy
Starting Out
The Arctic Grail
The Great Depression
Niagara: A History of the Falls
My Times: Living with History
1967, The Last Good Year

Picture Books
The New City (with Henri Rossier)
Remember Yesterday
The Great Railway
The Klondike Quest
Pierre Berton's Picture Book
    of Niagara Falls
Winter
The Great Lakes
Seacoasts
Pierre Berton's Canada

Anthologies
Great Canadians
Pierre and Janet Berton's Canadian
    Food Guide
Historic Headlines
Farewell to the Twentieth Century
Worth Repeating
Welcome to the Twenty-first
    Century

Fiction
Masquerade (pseudonym
    Lisa Kroniuk)

Books for Young Readers
The Golden Trail
The Secret World of Og
Adventures in Canadian History
    (22 volumes)

WELCOME
TO THE
TWENTY-FIRST CENTURY

More Absurdities of Our Time

PIERRE BERTON

Doubleday Canada

Copyright © 1999 Pierre Berton Enterprises Ltd.

All rights reserved. The use of any part of this publication reproduced, transmitted, in any form or by any means, electronic, mechanical, photocopying, recording, or otherwise, or stored in a retrieval system, without the prior consent of the publisher – or, in case of photocopying or other reprographic copying, a licence from the Canadian Reprography Collective – is an infringement of the copyright law.

Canadian Cataloguing in Publication Data

Berton, Pierre, 1920–
    Welcome to the twenty-first century

ISBN 0-385-25817-8

1. Popular culture – Canada – History – 20th century. 2. Popular culture – United States – History – 20th century. 3. Canada – Social life and customs – 20th century.* 4. United States – Social life and customs – 20th century. I. Title.

FC89.B374 1999   306.'0971'0904   C99-930918-8
F1021.2.B374 1999

Jacket photograph by Denise Grant
Jacket and text design by Joseph Gisini /Andrew Smith Graphics Inc.
Printed and bound in the USA

Published in Canada by
Doubleday Canada, a division of
Random House of Canada Ltd.
105 Bond Street
Toronto, Ontario
M5B 1Y3

BVG   10   9   8   7   6   5   4   3   2   1

CONTENTS

FOREWORD

GENTLE READER:

As I write these words (on an obsolete typewriter), we have less than a year to go—less than a year to cleanse our memories of the absurdities of the past and welcome a pristine future, happily free of the imbecilities that have been our lot over the past decades.

Millenniums do that—or so we are led to believe. When the hands of the Big Clock reach midnight, we convince ourselves that a shiny new world awaits—a world magically free of such irritants as national separatist movements, Cold War nonsense, commercialized Yules, overblown Royal Tours, mail-order junk, unreadable best-sellers, and recycled television series—all of which are dissected on the pages that follow.

"Welcome," we cry, breathing a sigh of relief as the New Age arrives. The follies of the past are behind us, and good riddance, too.

Or are they? The absurd is ever-present and not to be expunged by the flip of a calendar page. In this slim volume, you will note, I have chronicled certain examples of the twentieth-century huckster's art that we now call the Hard Sell. It is pleasant to suppose that in the coming century it will go the way of Lucky Strike Green, but I suspect it will continue to flourish, like the Incredible Snowstorm Plant depicted on page 62.

For as the millennium approaches, we fail to recognize

that the hardest sell of all has been the selling of the Millennium itself.

In one sense the New Age has already arrived. So much has changed, sometimes even for the better! How many of us are left to sing the lyrics of one of the hurtin' songs of the late fifties? For that matter, how many of us want to? That's progress of a kind.

We no longer talk about a "clean" H-bomb. And some of us are too young to remember when everybody did. It may be that in the new century the H-bomb will be as obsolete as Ann Landers, but I wouldn't bet on it. Still, there has been some progress. The oldsters in the audience may recall that there was a time when packages of margarine were turned back at the Quebec border. In the twentieth century we got free trade with the United States. In the twenty-first we may even get free trade within Canada.

Only the senior citizens will remember a time when we worried about American influences in our culture. They still exist in spades—but who worries any more? Superman no longer dominates the comic pages, but he remains a cultural icon thanks to the movies, while Perry Mason has been immortalized by TV's never-ending reruns. We've lost Buck Rogers, but we've still got *Star Trek*. When the new century gets going we can expect to see the same kind of thing in 3-D (without the funny glasses).

By the end of the twenty-first century two products that we once thought of as all-enduring will surely be extinct. I refer to tobacco and royalty. Indeed, it may well be noted at the turn of the new century that the era's greatest triumph was to outlaw, not war, but smoke. Cigarettes will be viewed as anachronisms of the past; so will the smoke-and-mirrors act we call the Royal Family.

Let me take you back almost half a century and quote from a motivational report made for the DuMaurier cigarette people. Motivational reports were very big in the twentieth century; people practically set their watches by them. In this report the motivational researchers attempted to find out what kind of people smoked DuMauriers. I quote it word for word, just as it was prepared for Imperial Tobacco. It is so extraordinary that I have to assure all and sundry that the quote is absolutely correct:

The DuMaurier smokers like to think of themselves as being a distinctive group of people. They pride themselves on being different from the average type of guy, and superior to him or her in sensitivity and discrimination. Attributes like broadmindedness, being cosmopolitan and artistic, are highly valued. It is important to them to try anything new. They feel that they are modern enough to be able to enjoy it.

As a whole, these smokers are rather forceful. They appear in the interviews as the "thinking" type of person, perhaps above the average level of intelligence, who is able to contemplate the different situations and their details and approach in a versatile and lively manner.

However, they do not represent a group of easy-going people. Their actions are in general of a highly tense nature. Their anxiety is not particularly focused at a specific object, like for instance at aggression or sexual experiences, but is underlying and permeates most of their actions.

The emotional responses of the smokers exhibit also a certain diffuseness. They are free-floating and easily aroused. Hence, emotions are readily attached to almost all situations these smokers picture.

This underlying feeling of anxiety tends to make them careful in all life areas—one has to be on guard continually to make the best of things. This attitude is apparent in regard to their smoking. Although these men are not particularly anxious about their health, they feel at the same time that it would be unwise to look for extra trouble and in this respect the safeguard of the filter cigarette is important to them.

Social contacts are very important to these smokers insofar as these may be an indication of relative status. Since they like to think of themselves as distinctive and as set apart from others, they are very much aware of things going on around them and sensitive in their social relations. Consequently, their social interactions are often not without strain.

The opinion the non-smokers have of DuMaurier corresponds rather closely to that of the smokers; however, they consider it on the whole a more extreme cigarette. . . . Its high social status brands it in their opinion as the cigarette for social climbers and snobbish types, or, in a more positive sense, as the brand for smart and intelligent people. On the one hand the non-smokers feel admiration for the DuMaurier smokers who seem to them to be usually the successful people; on the other hand they resent their standoffishness.

Does anybody take this sort of nonsense seriously? Apparently, yes. The big shots did back then before the cancer scare was properly underway. It's the sort of thing that might easily provoke a letter to Ann Landers:

DEAR ANN LANDERS:

I'm in trouble. Recently, I started going out with the sweetest imaginable boy. Only one thing bothers me about him. You see, he smokes DuMaurier cigarettes.

I, personally, do not smoke and so am able to look at the situation objectively. Certainly I feel a great admiration for my boyfriend, for he is unusually successful and yet, on the other hand, I find myself occasionally resenting his stand-offishness. His habit of blowing smoke through his nostrils when I introduce him to my parents, and shouting "Peasants!"—well, I must confess, this irritates me.

I should add, too, that his social interactions are not without strain. I didn't particularly care for the way he butted his DuMaurier on my little three-year-old brother the other day, simply because he felt the ashtrays in our home were *de trop*, as he puts it.

And yet the thing I love about him, Ann, is his sensitivity and discrimination. He discriminates against almost everybody, especially "the average type of guy," the Players smokers and other low social orders.

One thing that bothers me, though, are his social responses, which exhibit a certain diffuseness. The way he'll puff on his DuMaurier and eye other girls, for instance. He tells me his emotions are free-floating and easily aroused and that it's important to him to try everything new. I tell you, Miss Landers, this has me worried.

Please advise me. What should I do? Should I accept him

just as he is—cosmopolitan, artistic, mixed-up—or should I fight like a mad dog to get him to switch to Rothmans?

Yours in perplexity,
Gloria Whirm

The obvious answer in these stern times would be for Ann to tell her to make him quit smoking. But that wasn't an accepted solution in the mid-twentieth century. Tobacco companies spent big bucks on magazine, newspaper, and television advertising. To demand that this hucksterism cease would have been almost as shocking as suggesting that the Royal Family, like a DuMaurier, was obsolete. That was sheer blasphemy, as Miss Joyce Davidson, the TV hostess, discovered.

It's hard to believe now, but Miss Davidson was deprived temporarily of her livelihood and subjected to the hundred-thousand-watt glare of front-page publicity because, for the first time in her life, she ventured to offer an opinion of sorts in public. What was Miss Davidson's heinous crime? Did she attack the sexual mores of her time? Certainly not. Did she confess that she was a member of the international Communist conspiracy? No-o! Did she say that Canadian hockey was a brutal sport, like wrestling, and ought to be abolished? Not a bit of it. Hers was a graver offence. On Dave Garroway's *Today* show *she just didn't appear to be as emotionally enthusiastic about royal tours as the press felt she should be. And she, a CBC icon!*

At school, her two small girls heard their mother called "pig" and "traitor" because Miss Davidson refused to give a phony answer to a candid question.

Members of the public demanded her head for treason. Others insisted she be fired. As a result, Miss Davidson was not seen on television that week.

She was scheduled to be seen on the CBC's *Tabloid*, on which she was a regular host and had every intention of appearing. But when she arrived at the studio directly from New York, she was met in the hall by Mr. Fergus Mutrie, Director of TV Operations for Ontario. A short, rather embarrassed conversation took place.

Mr. Mutrie might have said, "Joyce, a lot of people have been phoning us demanding that you be fired because you voiced an opinion on NBC. Well, thank God, this is a free country where a man or a woman—even a TV interviewer— can say what he pleases. We don't intend to be pressured on this matter, so go on in there and do your stuff."

But Mr. Mutrie did not say this. If Mr. Mutrie had raised a silver bugle to his lips and blown the retreat he couldn't have made himself more clear. It might be better, said Mr. Mutrie, if she didn't go on *Tabloid*, what with feeling running so high. It would be in her own best interests and probably in the best interests of the program. Miss Davidson, who was feeling pretty dispirited at this point, agreed.

All that day the wires between Ottawa and Toronto had been humming on the general topic of What Shall We Do with Joyce? Miss Davidson now learned that there were to be weekend discussions about her fate. When she saw the handwriting on the wall, she gave in.

At this point the CBC might have said, "Leave of absence? Why that would be an admission that this isn't a free country! That would be a clear warning to anybody else who dares to venture an unorthodox opinion that he'd better think twice before speaking out! On the contrary, you'll go on *Tabloid* next week and do two interviews a night instead of one, as if nothing whatever had happened."

But the poor, miserable, wretched, spineless, harried CBC, bullied by parliamentary committees, badgered by back-benchers, bludgeoned by a provincial premier, sniped at by TV critics and editorial writers, heckled by private broadcasters, harassed by religious pressure groups, and finally driven into a blue funk by 593 phone calls—the pitiable, tormented, gutless CBC blew out such a sigh of relief that, I am informed, the windows on Jarvis Street rattled clear down to the Frontenac Arms.

I wonder what the reaction would have been if Miss Davidson's opinions had been on some less sacrosanct subject. Suppose, for instance, she had told Mr. Garroway that she no longer found she could believe in God and was, therefore, an atheist. I doubt if the remark would have got more than a few inches in the TV columns, let alone an unctuous lecture from the mayor.

But Miss Davidson's atheism was of a higher and more alarming order. You could get away with a disbelief of God in those days, but don't try to run against the new religion—the Royalty Cult. There lay the real blasphemy.

Actually, Miss Davidson's remarks were not anti-royal. She was merely bored by Royal Tours, which is a somewhat different thing.

She said, "I think I feel the way most Canadians feel [about the Royal Tour]—indifferent. I think at the time of the first visit I was excited . . . but the average Canadian, I think, is pretty indifferent to this one. . . ."

This blasphemy was rendered more heinous because it was uttered on foreign soil. The one thing we had that the Americans didn't have was a queen—we've always felt pretty smug about that. They had the Empire State Building, the New York Yankees, Marilyn and General Motors, but we had a girl in a golden Cadillac with a plastic bubble, so there! And now along came Joyce, downgrading it all with a single sentence.

That was one reason for the vituperation heaped on Miss Davidson's head. The other was that there was considerable truth in what she said.

That afternoon radio station CHUM opened all of its phone lines after asking its listeners to call in and answer this question: "Are most Canadians indifferent to the Royal Tour or are they interested in the Royal Tour?"

The results (before the Bell Telephone Company asked the station to cry halt): INDIFFERENT: 628; INTERESTED: 327.

The unreported, unheralded, and unpublicized truth was that, after five Royal Tours, a good number of Canadians were weary of the endless bickerings and squabblings among petty officials as to who should shake hands with whom; weary of imagined slights on the part of small towns and villages; weary of the Niagara of fatuous trivia that poured from Royal Tour reporters; weary of Prince Philip's endless and inevitable spats with the photographers; weary of the long lists of upper-class, non-union Anglo-Saxons invited to Tour banquets; weary of rented toppers and practised curtsies and inane speeches of welcome and awestruck radio commentators and

gushy women reporters and meaningless illuminated address-
es and all the other appurtenances that caparison the studied
ritual dance we call a Royal Tour. I liked the first one fine. But
in spite of official protestations that each succeeding one
would be "different," I quickly discovered that if you'd seen
one, you'd seen them all.

How long ago it all seems! How ancient! Yet some of us
old fogeys—those of us, say, who have reached fifty or
more—may remember the incident and ask ourselves how that
could have happened. Miss Davidson's story sounds like some
of the more fanciful fables that appear in the pages that follow.

All, I must insist, bespeak a greater truth.

The old institutions are eroding. The Cold War, which
once scared the pants off us, has vanished. Weapons of mass
destruction still exist, but they aren't used. Why bother?
We've done very well, thank you, in Rwanda and Serbia
using tried and true methods.

How will those who follow come to define the twenty-
first century? As the era of the *Harder* Sell? Or will it become
the Age of Cynicism brought on by grasping politicians, lying
propagandists, and a subservient media dedicated to papering
over the true absurdities of our time? If I had said that earlier in this century I'd have been reviled as a Red—a "Godless
Communist," to use the accepted epithet. Today, as a new century dawns, people no longer live in terror of the Reds—or
the blacks, either, for that matter. We can pretty well say what
we wish, absurd or not, even if it flies in the face of the gospel
of political correctness. And in that change, perhaps, lies a
small beacon of hope.

One

THE VIEW FROM THE TWENTY-FIRST CENTURY

Memories of the
Age of Violence

To those of us who have been studying the Twentieth Century, here in our course on ancient social cultures, it comes as no surprise to learn that the era was one of unparalleled brutality.

Indeed, the public was fed a diet of organized ruffianism, perhaps as a sop to its otherwise wretched existence. The sports of those days were, by our standards, ferocious and cruel. One of the most popular, known as "boxing," involved the spectacle of two men pummelling each other into insensibility. The winner was expected to achieve victory by actually beating his adversary into unconsciousness by repeated blows upon the head.

Lest the contestants tire before one succumbed, breathing spaces were allowed at regular intervals while each of the mauled gladiators was partially resuscitated. Many men paid as much as a day's wages to watch these spectacles.

It is significant that a companion sport known as "wrestling," wherein two contestants grappled away, attempting to throw each other on the ground, was so tame by comparison that in order to enliven it the contestants often simulated actual pain by tortured screams and facial contortions, in order to satisfy the spectators.

On the North American continent, whose people considered themselves the most advanced in the world, two other ferocious sports were allowed to go unchecked: "hockey," in which rival players attacked each other with crooked sticks, and "football," in which the contestants kicked ostensibly at a ball but in reality at each other. In another game, "baseball," the spectators themselves became contestants, shrieking imprecations at the players and flinging missiles at the unfortunate whose duty it was to keep the opponents from flying at each other's throats.

Death and violent injury were woven like bloody threads into the sombre fabric that formed the backdrop of existence away back in the Twentieth Century. Because of the primitive nature of the vehicles, travel was a cat-and-mouse affair. Those people who still used their legs to propel themselves were called "pedestrians," and the literature of the times shows them in constant rivalry with the "motorists," who drove the hand-operated "automobiles." No day passed in any country[1] that did not see dozens maimed or killed in public by the wheeled machines.

These were operated freely by the insane, the addle-brained, the neurotic and the sick, and, as the control of each device depended solely on the whims of the operator and not at all on any scientifically determinable force, the havoc was almost unimaginable. Some cities indeed had actual death charts placed in prominent places listing the score of those killed. One of these may still be seen at the Rondex Institute from behind a radiation shield.

Yet twentieth-century man seems to have adopted a fatalistic attitude to death. Ignoring "intersections"—crude paths cleared at periodic intervals from moving traffic—he dodged

---

[1] The twentieth-century world was parcelled into separate anarchic units whose boundaries had been arrived at romantically.

helter-skelter between the snorting machines, while the drivers zigzagged among one another in a reckless harum-scarum. Those few motion pictures that have been preserved unclouded give a jerky, neurotic movement to the two-dimensional images of the time.

It was, however, his treatment of the sick and the insane that puts the stamp of brutality on the Twentieth Century. The standard treatment of many of the sick was imprisonment, and these unfortunate sufferers were actually known as "prisoners." Whenever a man's illness demonstrated itself in theft or violence, as it often did in that violent age, he was locked in a barred cell, sometimes for a lifetime, without medical treatment of any kind.

The people of that time responded to violence with more violence, and the principle of revenge (they called it a "deterrent") ruled. Sexual invalids were flogged with a knotted thong or leather strap, then often set free to commit further offences. Murderers were exterminated, not cured, and in the crudest manner—often by having their necks broken at the end of a length of rope by which they were dangled from a high place.

Before being killed, these wretches were driven half crazy by being left for months in a solitary cell to contemplate their end. A peculiar form of torture known as a "stay of execution" was in vogue. The method was to postpone the condemned man's execution for brief periods to increase his mental anguish.

Although he tended to treat cancer and TB[2] sufferers with a solicitude that at all times bordered on the sentimental,

---

[2] Diseases of the age, now unknown.

twentieth-century man failed utterly to understand, diagnose or cure the major illnesses of the mind whose manifestations were what he would have called "crimes against society." For simpler diseases there were hospitals of a sort, for the more serious ones only jails and death cells. These sufferers were looked upon with universal loathing, distrust and hatred. It was commonly held that their maladies were their own fault. Few realized that each was suffering in some measure from a disease that he could only dimly diagnose—the disease of the century itself.

The dilemma was a familiar one: a primitive people had become devilishly clever with their hands, but the implications of what they had wrought only bewildered them. The motor car was a good example. Those who developed this crude and wasteful vehicle did not foresee the problem. The roads and highways were little more than smoothed-over remnants of the wagon age. By mid-century, people contemplated the paradoxical spectacle of themselves crawling by inches toward the ever-expanding limits of their city at a speed that was often little better than that of a nineteenth-century trotting horse.

Such minor irritations they solved in a makeshift fashion. But these were only symbols of a greater dilemma of the same order that rose to plague them. Dimly the people of those days realized that atomic development could not be allowed to progress as haphazardly as earlier scientific inventions. And yet they were as children, groping in the dark, blindly seeking a solution that evaded them.

Alas, for those who followed, the rest of that terrible story is now ancient history.

Memories of the
Age of Noise

If a being from our own time were suddenly plucked from his home and set down abruptly in what the people of that day called the Twentieth Century (the new calendar had not been adopted), his first reaction would certainly be one of stark terror. Indeed, it is doubtful if he could long survive the nerve-shattering and unceasing clamour that more than anything else marked the short[1] existence of every man, woman and child in that unhappy era.

This incessant din, which followed twentieth-century man from street to office to home, which tormented his rest and maddened his working hours, was perhaps the most significant thing about these times. Men were emerging from the initial stages of an industrial revolution, but they had as yet failed to tame one of its ugliest by-products: noise. It was an Age of Noise.

Historians now believe that the people of those days dimly realized that noise is a poison that destroys the intellectual processes: recent excavations in the old city of Toronto have uncovered from the ruins of a public library signs urging "QUIET." And there must have been some understanding of the connection between noise and illness since the approaches to the hospitals appear to have been lined with tiny ineffectual placards pleading for quiet for the patients within.

---

[1] Men of seventy were considered old and in many countries received an "old-age" pension.

Yet the larger implications of this escaped the sub-man of the Twentieth Century, for he continued to place the hospitals in the centre of his ugly, clamorous cities. And although his mental institutions were overflowing, he failed to notice the connection between the ear-splitting racket of daily life and the problem of mental illness.

It is quite impossible for us to comprehend the clamour of those far-off times. The people of that era seemed inured to it. Indeed, it is doubtful if many of them realized that the air around them was never silent.

Twentieth-century man awoke to the rude jangle of an automatic clockwork bell, shaved to the racking buzz of an electric razor in his ears,[2] and drove himself to work with a steady stream of gas explosions pounding around him. The public conveyances, which like the hand-operated vehicles travelled almost invariably above ground, were even noisier and more congested.

In their offices, the people of the Twentieth Century attracted attention by sounding a buzzer or ringing a bell.[3] Indeed, it was an age of bells. Schools and churches gathered people to them by ringing a bell. Telephone calls, which were based purely on sound and not on sight, were opened by the shrill ringing of a bell.[4] Locomotives, streetcars, bicycles and the various other primitive means of transport all carried bells.

---

[2] No method of killing hair follicles at birth had been discovered.

[3] Extrasensory perception was entirely unknown.

[4] It is perhaps significant that these telephones were actually called "Bell Telephones."

In the homes, thin partitions failed to keep more than a few decibels of sound from the living quarters. Twentieth-century women attempted to clean their floor coverings with a "vacuum cleaner," a machine that according to the literature of the day seems to have been a synonym for noise.

In the background, the radio—a device that was based entirely on sound and was allowed to operate untrammelled by any authority—kept up a ceaseless and unnerving racket in every home, conveyance and public place. Every radio and every television set had a device attached to it known as a "*loud*speaker." It is interesting to note that the emphasis was on the first syllable.

The streets, as can be imagined, were a constant bedlam. All vehicular traffic, which was of the most congested and unwieldy nature, ran freely at street level. None of it was silent. Thus, the air was constantly rent with the hoot and clang of horns and bells that warned the luckless foot traveller[5] that a conveyance was bearing down upon him. In this way the idea of noise was inseparably connected with the idea of fear.

A passenger travelling by air found it impossible to talk below a shout, so great was the racket generated by the engines of the day. Overland "trains," which often took two to four days to reach their destination, roared across the country shattering the sleep and peace of mind of those who lived beside the right-of-way. Even the rivers and lakes, and the ocean bays, so quiet in our times, were rendered unspeakably

---

[5] A great many people actually walked many dozens of yards by using their legs in a sort of see-saw motion to propel themselves.

ugly by the constant hoots and shrieks and put-put-puts of the water traffic of the era.

Buildings were torn down and re-erected to the accompaniment of a cacophony that even the reports of those times agree were nerve-shattering.

That twentieth-century man was vaguely aware of this is seen in the archaeologists' discoveries of early "soundproofing" apparatus—desperate attempts to cushion some of the "offices"[6] from the ever-present noise. Some cities even had "noise campaigns" in which trucks with loudspeakers roared about the streets urging more quiet. These proved totally useless. Small wonder, then, that the newspapers of the day were crammed with advertisements for headache cures. Indeed, many of these cures were based on the speed with which a throbbing head pain could be dulled. Large sums were spent on medical research as men, women and children demanded faster and faster relief.

And yet, in spite of these token obeisances to the Goddess of Silence, the people of those far-off times actually seemed to have been drugged by noise. Like drug addicts, they craved more. Nostalgic references to the "cry of the city" occur in much of the literature of the time. The music of the day was extremely noisy as anyone who has studied the works of Igor Stravinsky, a minor composer then held in high esteem, will testify. The folk music grew louder and more raucous as each decade passed, and the very names

---

[6] Tiny cell-like compartments where middle-class males spent half their waking hours.

applied to it were onomatopoeic in their harshness and explosiveness: *jazz, bop, rock* and so on.

It is impossible to believe now, but one breakfast food was actually sold because it was noisy. Its promoters claimed that it went "snap, crackle, pop." And one medicine was advertised solely on the basis of its loud fizz, a sound that was amplified many times over on the loudspeakers.

And that was how it was, away back then.

Memories of the
Age of Grime

Well, students, once again, here in our Ancient Social History course, we are going to deal with that troubled and primitive era, the Twentieth Century.

As we have already noted, this was the Age of Noise. But it was also the Age of Filth . . . the Age of Ugliness . . . the Age of Uniformity, when all but the upper classes lived in identical houses that squatted almost wall to wall, row upon row, dangerously close together along the narrow, uninviting streets, thus giving a monotonously depressing air to the dark, crowded cities.

The largest cities were, for the most part, devoid of foliage or plant life of any kind. From the air, they appeared as ugly scars on the landscape. Twentieth-century man gazed out from his small windows onto a vista augmented by a tangle of wires, poles, chimneys, clotheslines, fences and soft-drink signs.

For sheer ugliness, the dwelling places knew no parallel. Many of them were actually built of small gobbets of baked clay, each pasted together to produce a virtually windowless shell in which the people existed.

The uniformity of the furnishings was such that a University of Chicago anthropologist was able to boast that he could walk down any Midwestern street and, merely by looking at the exterior of each house, tell accurately the salary, temperament, and personal tastes of the dweller; and the uniformity of thinking was such that an official of the "Gallup" poll could say with certainty that once you knew a person's sex, language, income and geographical location, you could guess, eight times out of ten, how he or she would think on any given subject.

In those days, people often judged beauty in terms of shininess. They shined their cars, floors, hair, and their plumbing fixtures. Goods were often rendered more saleable because they had some shiny objects attached to them (a bathtub with chrome fixtures, for example). And many of the public places where people gathered to become intoxicated were made more desirable by the addition of shiny metallic furniture and walls. It was an age of tinsel glitter, and yet underneath it all, it was an age of indescribable filth.

Dirt was everywhere. The gas-propelled vehicles were equipped with shielding devices aptly named "mudguards," which warded off flying filth that littered the streets. Dogs, cats—even the occasional horse—wandered freely through the thoroughfares, depositing their excrement on roadway and sidewalk.

Few householders had built-in methods of destroying garbage, and the accumulated refuse of the kitchens was dumped unceremoniously into vessels known as "garbage cans," which sat out in muddy lanes until workers paid for the purpose spilled out the fly-infested contents into vehicles that were driven unguarded through the streets.

The whole was often dumped into the sea or the waterways to pollute the shores and beaches, many of which were condemned for sanitary reasons, as were the streams into which the underground sewage was allowed to flow.

The filth of the streets was beyond belief. Fewer than half of the thoroughfares were paved and then only imperfectly.

Gaping holes, cracks and imperfections in the pavement served as dirt catchers and receptacles for the oil and grease that spewed from the engines of the vehicles. The cement was impossible to clean, though there was really very little attempt at cleaning, anyway.

The exteriors of most buildings were porous and grooved so that they quickly became encrusted by the cloud of smoke and pollution that hung over the cities like a pall—blotting out the sun, choking the citizenry, and befouling the land. As there were no laws dealing with the cleaning of buildings, most structures in the heart of the cities quickly turned black. Indeed, it was said to be a mark of pride with certain banks to refuse to have their buildings cleaned with steam on the theory that the accumulation of grime somehow lent the institution a certain solidity.

Interiors were equally dirty. Those photos which have not been destroyed by radiation show that the favourite theme of the amateur photographer was the capturing of beams of dust motes slanting down through the windows of a church, railway station or other public building. The housewife's main method of cleaning her floors (a task made difficult by the existence of thick, dust-catching "carpets") was to use the "vacuum-cleaner," an incredible device that attempted to suck the dust up into a sack. Paradoxically, the sackful of dust was deposited in the garbage can where, inevitably, great quantities of it swirled back into the common air.

The result of all this was that man himself was dirty. Advertisements of the day show this better than anything else. Again and again they stress human uncleanliness and exhort the people to great lengths to achieve a well-scrubbed state that was apparently unattainable. The most widely used method was to suspend dirt particles in an emulsion and wash them away with running water. The emulsion was produced by a substance called "soap" that would today be classed as an irritant. But the literature of the time urged everyone to make use of this cure-all.

Reading between the lines of these ads, we see the twentieth-century man emerge as a hairy and unclean animal, foul-breathed, yellow-toothed and odoriferous, his pores heavy with grime, his hair weighted with grease. His womenfolk are pictured as even more repulsive: their clothing soiled so quickly that three out of four prominent medical authorities, quoted again and again, exhorted them to rinse these garments thoroughly each night.

Perhaps this explains why the era was disease-ridden. Human resistance was so low that a slight chill brought it below the point where the system could effectively fight viruses. This produced a disease colloquially called "the cold." Its spread was abetted by the people themselves, who blew catarrh into pieces of cloth that they carried about in their pockets. The virus was so widespread that people referred to the "common" cold, and there was no gathering of twenty or more that was not marked by the continual sniffling, coughing, wheezing, sneezing, and snorting that were the audible signs of a universal affliction.

That was what it was like, students, back in the Dark Ages. In retrospect it may seem a romantic period, but when you look at it critically it was nothing of the kind.

Nightmares of the
Next Century

It was not until the twenty-first century that the subdivisions began to cause real trouble. Until that time they had been merely a nuisance, spreading out from the every-expanding cities in concentric circles, the lots growing tinier by the decade.

In 2010, the first of the farmers' riots occurred on the outskirts of Winnipeg, a few miles from Regina. The immediate cause was a new subdivision, five hundred miles long, straddling the Trans-Canada Highway and containing more than a quarter of a million identical machine-made homes, all on twenty-foot lots. It was hailed by the mayor of Winnipeg as "a milestone in progress." But it raised the assessment value of the neighbouring farmland so much that the crushing burden of taxes made agriculture impossible.

The revolt was quickly quelled by the RCMP, but it touched off further disturbances all over North America. A subdivider who had bulldozed a forest area near the city limits of Toronto (not far from Peterborough) narrowly escaped lynching. At Trois-Rivières, a suburb of Montreal, a group of malcontents led a spirited attack on bulldozers and destroyed three with Molotov cocktails. The attack, alas, came too late to save the topsoil, which had already been pushed into the St. Lawrence.

In 2015 the mayor of Greater Toronto proudly announced that the city had reached a total population of five million. This huge consumer market, he said, ensured the prosperity of the Queen City, which had outstripped the rosiest predictions of the demographers. A few people complained about the price of bread, which had risen to five dollars a loaf because of the wheat scarcity, and there was some nostalgia, too, for the good old days of green vegetables. But it was generally agreed that the draining of the Holland Marsh and its conversion into a popular midtown apartment district had been a magnificent engineering feat. As the mayor said in his statement, "You just can't stop progress."

In August 2019 two curiously isolated incidents occurred that, in retrospect, take on considerable significance. In New York City a green salad went on display in a department store window. The oddity attracted such crowds that police had to be called to get traffic moving. In Toronto, in the congested Don Mills slum district, a woman appeared on the street with six children, all her own. She was hissed at and spat upon by the neighbours.

- In 2021, the first of the twenty-two-lane highways was completed between New York and Chicago. It was designed for a speed of 100 mph, but the traffic was so heavy on all twenty-two lanes that a limit of 15 mph had to be set.

- In 2024, the Toronto subway was completed to Barrie, and no automobiles were allowed within the city, whose limits began at the first subway exit. A special traffic detail was appointed to control the heavy pedestrian traffic, which moved in designated lanes along the former Highways 400 and 401, now converted into giant shopping malls.

- In 2025, Loblaws announced the construction of the world's largest supermarket, a giant edifice designed to enclose, under a single roof, the space once occupied by the old municipality of Swansea. The supermarket took in a former building that had taken up the entire space once occupied by High Park.

- In 2027, access to the few remaining parks in the greater Toronto area was rationed. Special tickets were provided on a monthly basis, and each citizen was allowed two hours to stroll in the greenery. Queues several miles long formed before the gates for this privilege. The gates were guarded by machine-guns.

- In 2029, the province of Ontario, following the lead of several U.S. states, banned all house building within its boundaries. A subdividers' lobby fought the legislation, but it was upheld by the Supreme Court in 2031. Special police details were appointed to ferret out house bootleggers attempting to construct log cabins at astronomical prices along the Canadian Shield.

- In 2034, in an unprecedented announcement from Buckingham Palace, the young king stated that he would limit his family to a single heir and called upon all patriotic Britons to follow suit. A campaign of vilification against people with large families was stepped up in the popular press.

- By 2037, most countries of the world had made it illegal to have more than three children. Three years later it became illegal to have more than two children. By 2045 there were only three countries left—Paraguay, Ghana, and Liechtenstein—where it was legal for a family to have more than a single child.

By 2047, every country in the world except Madagascar had outlawed the building of single, detached homes and had made the occupation of any existing detached dwelling by a single family a serious crime. In Victoria, B.C., that year, a Horace J. Simpkins was sentenced to seven years' imprisonment because he, his wife, two children, mother-in-law and maiden aunt had occupied a four-room bungalow by themselves—this group being designated by the courts as a "family unit." The children were given three years definite and two years indefinite in the provincial reformatory. The judge, in his summing up, castigated the Simpkinses for having two children.

In 2049, the United States and Canada enacted federal laws making the birth of any child without a licence a crime. This was hailed as a "far-reaching piece of social legislation" by progressive elements.

In 2051, in Chicago, the first mile-high apartment house was completed to house 2,500 family units. Two hundred similar structures were in the construction stage. That same year multiple-dwelling life became compulsory in ten U.S. and three Canadian cities.

In 2054, Canada's population having reached a total of 156 millions, the federal government made all births illegal and suspended permits. New legislation was enacted providing for the extermination of all children born illegally and special "extermination depots" were set up across the country to administer the matter efficiently. A special detachment of the RCMP was formed to delve into the backgrounds of all families to determine the number of illegal children. In the first six months, the bureau of statistics reported that a total of 250,000 children between the ages of one week and twelve years had been exterminated.

The report was considered most encouraging since this figure represented a healthy 4.3 percent of the number of people who had died during the same period of starvation or trampling.

"We are," said the prime minister of the day, "well on the road to coming to grips with the population explosion."

Two

THE CANADIAN WAY OF LIFE

Announcing a National
Separatist Movement

Dr. Bourassa Grebe, the well-known Canadian nationalist, announced today the formation of an All-Canada Separatist Movement to co-ordinate and channel the work of various local and provincial separatist and secessionist movements springing up across the Dominion.

The following groups are being approached to affiliate with the national organization:

- The Quebec separatist movement (designed to convert French-speaking Canada into an independent Republic of Laurentia);
- The Victoria, B.C., secessionist movement, designed to bring freedom to the oppressed Vancouver Islanders and make the island a separate Crown colony with its own distinctive flag (a Union Jack);
- The Duncan, B.C., secessionist movement, pledged to bring about the secession of Duncan, B.C., from the rest of Vancouver Island;
- The Newfoundland Freedom and Anti-Baby-Bonus League, sworn to abolish all oppressive Ottawa domination and bring freedom back to Newfoundland;
- The Northern Ontario Independence Foundation, which is attempting to form a separate province on the Canadian Shield independent of the crushing heel of Queen's Park.

Although sympathizing with the aims of these various

groups, Dr. Grebe believes that they are looking at the matter of secession from too local a point of view.

"They are putting the cart before the horse," he declared at a press conference this morning. "The first object of our national movement must be to obtain our independence from the United States.

"We will have to move cautiously, of course. Our immediate goal is simply to get complete autonomy within the North American framework. But our ultimate goal is out-and-out secession—even to the extent of having our own distinctive Canadian foreign policy."

Once Canada becomes an independent country with its own culture, its own traditions, its own values and its own language, it will be time enough to encourage further separatist movements, Dr. Grebe explained.

"When that proud day arrives," he declared, "then the other groups who make up the national body can, of course, secede from each other. After all, nothing succeeds like secession."

The All-Canada Separatist Movement's first venture, Dr. Grebe announced, would be to establish a Distinctive Canadian Cola Drink.

"What we are trying to achieve," he said, "is a beverage redolent of the Canadian way of life, something that will evoke the pungency of, say, burning maple leaves, or, if you will, burning books."

After that, the Movement will work to abolish all American TV and radio networks in Canada.

"It is our plan to replace the Canadian Broadcasting

Corporation with a network providing distinctively Canadian programs," Dr. Grebe explained. "I know that this is a novel concept, but strong measures are going to be needed if we are to secede."

Dr. Grebe admitted that the Movement's avowed goal of getting Canadian textbooks into the schools to replace U.S.-manufactured texts posed an extremely difficult problem, but he felt that it was one that was not insoluble.

Visionaries in the Movement even predict a distinctive Canadian Parliament and look forward to an era when Canadians will no longer vote in the U.S. presidential elections or take part in U.S. political conventions as has been the trend in recent years.

"As we see it, the new Parliament will be entirely independent of the Congress," Dr. Grebe declared. "We hope to establish an independent Prime Minister, an independent cabinet and even—though this is admittedly a difficult problem—an independent Department of External Affairs.

"I can even foresee a day when Canada will have its own representatives at the United Nations," Dr. Grebe said, and listeners could detect a quiver of emotion in his voice as he issued this surprising (and, to some, alarming) manifesto.

In speaking of the newly designed Parliament, Dr. Grebe made it clear that the present Upper House would be retained without change.

"It is generally agreed within the Movement that the Senate is one of the few distinctively Canadian institutions that we have," he pointed out. "There is nothing like it anywhere in the world."

The Movement's first goal, however, will be social and cultural rather than political or military.

"Much as we would like to free Baffin Island from U.S. armed occupation, we simply do not feel the time is ripe for overt action," Dr. Grebe said regretfully. "At the same time we want the freedom-loving people of Baffin to know that, when the moment comes, we are prepared to strike and strike hard against oppression."

Meanwhile, strong emphasis is to be placed by the Movement on a distinctive Canadian culture.

"If it develops that there is no distinctive Canadian culture (as seems likely), then it may become necessary to invent one," Dr. Grebe stated.

Canadians, he said, would be encouraged to speak, think, and write their own language. Indeed, at one time the Movement seriously considered a plan to convert the entire nation to a form of Quebec French. However, this met with strong opposition from the Quebec Separatists. They pointed out, with great logic, that if all Canadians spoke French their own attempts at secession could hardly be successful. As a result, the Movement has confined its efforts to a daring attempt to abolish the American "Z" from all Grade Three spelling classes.

Meanwhile, Dr. Grebe and his colleagues are working on a long-term plan to erect some sort of tariff wall between Canada and the United States as a first practical step to ultimate secession.

Such a wall was absolutely necessary, Dr. Grebe said, if this country is to develop and encourage local industry. He foresaw the day, for instance, when an independent Canada might even support a thriving textile industry, with looms in home workshops turning out simple garments of jute. Patriotic Canadians would be encouraged to wear this distinctive dress as a mark of their independence, he said.

Following Dr. Grebe's press conference, a second press conference was held by representatives of one of the affiliated groups—the Yellowknife and Coppermine Separatist Association—who outlined plans now under way to secede from the parent body.

Lecture Notes for an
All-Canadian Art Exhibit

The historical paintings that we have gathered together in this unique exhibition, friends and art lovers, are without doubt the very finest examples of genre painting in Canada. Taken together they provide a graphic social history of the nation. Say what you will about the Group of Seven; they certainly knew their Precambrian rock; but what did all those red maples, blasted pines, and gunmetal lakes tell us about the foibles of the people? In this new exhibition we are introduced to *real* Canadians, warts and all.

These works have one thing in common: they could only have been painted in this country—by Canadians and for Canadians. One doubts if any art lover in the Czech Republic, say, or Botswana, would get the point. Depicting as they do familiar scenes of Canadian life, they delineate as no other work can that inexpressible something which, for want of a better phrase, has been dubbed "The Canadian Way of Life— Past and Present."

Take for instance this magnificent canvas (No. 14 in your program) by Gastric Mundane, which he calls *Surrendering the Margarine at the Quebec Border.* Here is all the volatile exuberance of French-Canadian genre art at its best. Note the robust brush strokes used to portray the Quebec customs officers as they go whistling about their duties. Contrast the whiteness of the margarine with the scarlet of the visitors' faces as they are relieved of the contraband. Mundane's attention to small, seemingly unimportant detail is legend.

Notice in the shadows in the far right-hand corner that one customs officer, tempted to the point of near insanity, has actually tasted some of the forbidden food and is in the act of spitting it out onto the snow. The remorse that haunts his features is a triumph of the master's art. This great canvas is, of course, a companion piece to Mundane's folksier and more sentimental *Colouring the Margarine before Supper-time*, which now hangs in the Toronto Art Gallery.

Moving to the north wall we find a particularly impressive canvas by the great R.C. Victor, RCA. In this noble work, titled *Canadian Delegation Abstaining at the UN*, the artist manages to convey a feeling of calmness and lassitude which we have not seen in landscape art since the days of Corot and Millais. The work is revolutionary, however, in that it has been executed in a single colour, grey—a colour curiously appropriate to the occasion. The greying delegates in their grey, double-breasted suits with pearl grey cufflinks, look impassive and grey-faced as, arms folded, eyes closed, they keep their seats and their tempers while the storms of world politics revolve around them.

By contrast, the emotional canvas to the left (No. 91 in your booklets) has all the kaleidoscopic force we have come to associate with the work of Lignite Malfunction. Entitled *Aldermen's Wives Fainting during Royal Visit Ceremonies*, it depicts one of the more familiar scenes of Canadian life— and a memory which, no doubt, every school child cherishes. The crush of the crowd before the Toronto City Hall, the crisp efficiency of the St. John Ambulance men, the calmness of the mayor himself—all these are vividly depicted by

Malfunction's brush. Yet there is pathos here, too—note, for instance, the tiny little Union Jacks still clasped firmly in the insensible women's hands. The painting deserves to rank high with Malfunction's equally stark work, *The Bleeding Hockey Player.*

Sir Miles Truncheon's established masterpiece, *The Leave-Taking*, needs, of course, no introduction. No exhibit of Canadian painting would be complete without this moving canvas that has brought tears to the eyes of two generations of gallery-goers. The young boy about to set off for Toronto is shown hesitantly boarding the CPR flyer at Washbowl, Man., while his family, friends and well-wishers surround him. One of the local dignitaries is shown adjusting the blindfold and giving the youth a last cigarette as the porter motions him to come aboard. The young man seems to be saying that he will return, but the tears in the eyes of his mother indicate all too clearly the artist's belief that there is no return from Toronto.

On a happier note, we have in the Pachter Memorial Gallery, to our immediate right, Leadley Dirge's gay and stimulating watercolour, *An Old Canadian Custom*. It shows a pleasant family gathered in the parlour, busily designing Distinctive Canadian Flags. "Mom" is sewing hers into a sampler—a lively potpourri of maple leaves superimposed on a CBC-TV test pattern; Father, working at a drafting board, is trying for something more realistic: a Stars and Stripes with a small Union Jack in one corner; the kiddies are making their own flag designs with crayons. We did not need the artist to tell us that these designs along with thousands of others would be carefully packaged and sent in to the Central Committee on Flag Design, with copies to all the newspapers. Yet no hint of their ultimate rejection is to be seen in the eyes of the subjects. Not for nothing is Leadley Dirge known as the Canadian Breughel.

Now if you will follow me into the new wing I should like to show you the most truly magnificent painting in our collection—a masterly historical canvas of cyclopean proportions by the great Fitzhugh Vicarious, MBE. Commissioned at the last conference of Commonwealth Prime Ministers, it depicts the meeting of leaders of two of the oldest Commonwealth countries: Canada and South Africa. Mr. Vicarious, a shrewd judge of human nature, has not omitted the sly humour that was present on this occasion—a humour that does nothing to detract from the essential dignity of the moment. The late Mr. Diefenbaker is obviously having a "dig" at Mr. Verwoerd, no doubt for the latter's controversial policy of racial segregation. Chuckling genially, the Canadian leader is wagging his finger at the burly South African as if to say, in a joshing manner, "Naughty! Naughty!" Needless to say, Mr. Verwoerd is taking the ribbing in good part; the firm handclasp, the cheery smile, which the artist has depicted with such fidelity, show better than words that nothing can ever really mar Commonwealth relations. Mr. Vicarious' painting once again emphasizes the essential truth that Canadians are a moderate people.

We must pass quickly over several more notable canvases: Manley Outback's virile *Folk Dancing at Fillmore's*; Gabriel Steed's incisive study of *Jack Kent Cooke Taking the*

U.S. Oath of Allegiance; Fledgling Recoil's appealing portrayal of *The Cabinet Commuting a Child's Death Sentence.* All these historical works are in the finest tradition. More controversial, perhaps, is Painting No. 37, one of the few abstract works in the collection. Here a succession of whirling lines fly off the canvas in a variety of directions, providing a feeling of absolute anarchy and utter aimlessness. The viewer, indeed, will have difficulty in finding exactly where the painting is going and, as is usual in these cases, the title *Interchange on Highway 401* will give him very few clues. But for those whose interests lie in the realm of so-called nonobjective art, it will doubtless prove satisfactory.

Words of Caution to a Honeymooning Princess

The following document has been unearthed among the papers of Egerton Lascelles, equerry and confidant of Her Royal Highness, the Princess Margaret. The Princess had just announced her engagement to Anthony Armstrong-Jones, and the suggestion was that the happy couple might spend their honeymoon on Vancouver Island. Mr. Lascelles' reservations, which led to his instant dismissal, appear here for the very first time.

Your Royal Highness:

As you probably know, there is a certain local sentiment in favour of your spending your honeymoon in Canada. Several locations have been suggested: Lake Louise, Niagara Falls, an island off the B.C. coast, the Laurentian Hills, Wasaga Beach, etc. All of these spots have been frequented by honeymooners since the Iroquois scalped the Hurons, and I would not want in any way to deprecate their beauty or their charm.

But if you take my advice you will get as far away from Canada as possible. Run, do not walk, in the opposite direction. Go to the Himalayas—Everest if possible. Take a slow boat to Hong Kong, by way of Suez and Mandalay. Head for the Antarctic. But if you value your health, your peace of mind, your sanity and your future happiness, do not come to Canada.

Do not be misled by those siren voices from Ottawa and

points west that will tell you this is just the place for a quiet vacation. If you don't believe me, ask your sister. She and her husband once came here for what was to be a quiet vacation. When she got back home she had to take a real vacation to recover from it all.

Don't go for that tourist twaddle about a quiet little holiday on an island off the coast of B.C. Remember that to get to B.C., you will have to pass through Halifax, Saint John, Rimouski, Quebec City, Montreal, Ottawa, Toronto, Barrie, Stratford, Sudbury, Fort William, Winnipeg, Brandon, Regina, Saskatoon, Edmonton, Calgary, Field, Penticton, Vancouver, and Coppermine.

Don't think you can bypass them by taking the plane instead of the train. The plane will land at all these places. The mayor will make a speech and give you an illuminated address. A Brownie will give you a bouquet of flowers. Several natives will give you examples of native wickerwork. You will inspect the Girl Guides, the Wolf Cubs, the CGIT, and the Civil Defence. You will tour the veterans' hospitals where the veterans will give you a belt and wallets made of hand-tooled leather. The RCMP will beat up several photographers, providing a diversion for the crowd and the newspapers. There will then be a local festival that you must attend, since festivals are the rage over here these days. You will be expected to like the festival, which will start late and run till midnight, to be followed by a reception for the entire cast and their wives. The cast in each case will present you with a silver cigarette box with your name engraved on it so it can't be sold.

I had better warn you that by the time you reach Wetaskiwin (twenty-minute stop, inspection of Indian braves, brief speech of welcome, presentation of native beadwork) all hell will be breaking loose. There will be angry protests from the mayors of Red Deer, Chibougamau, Kitchener, Moncton, and Yellowknife because you have not visited their towns on your way to that little island off the B.C. coast. Your itinerary will be revised hastily to reroute you through these beauty spots.

You will meet a great many people on this nuptial journey, Princess. Most will be aldermen. Words cannot begin to describe the number of aldermen you will meet while on your honeymoon. There are several thousand in Toronto alone, and they and their wives will all be jammed together on the steps of our city hall when you pass through on your way to Point Pelee and Moosonee. We will try to arrange to have the sun shining brightly that day. Several dozen aldermen will faint from the heat and the excitement and the pre-royal-tour bracers, thus providing a fitting climax to a memorable day.

You will also have the prime minister with you, you lucky girl, you. Past indications suggest that he will get on the train at Halifax and stay until about New Westminster. He is great company on a honeymoon. When you are sitting out there on the rear platform with Tony, gazing at the prairie sunset, the prime minister will be on hand to regale you with exciting stories of the Old West: the defeat of Louis Riel, the defeat of Poundmaker, the defeat of Gabriel Dumont, the defeat of Mike Pearson and other legendary characters.

If you are really lucky you may also get George Pearkes when you hit the B.C. border. It's pretty well agreed up at Ottawa that George is a capital fellow for a royal tour. Get him going on the Bomarc missile; he is fascinating on that subject. It is all he talks about.

By the time you reach British Columbia there will be some newspaper talk about how tiring your honeymoon trip has been. Several reporters will claim you are on the verge of nervous collapse. The fact that your right arm is in a sling, that you have bandages on your ankles and are being pushed around in a wheelchair will lend a certain credence to these rumours. The papers will blame Ottawa officialdom for making the tour too strenuous. The mayor of Armpit, Sask., will issue a personal invitation for you to take a two-day rest at his town which, unaccountably, has been left off the itinerary. Don't go.

It will be announced, finally, that you are going to be allowed a well-earned rest of thirty-six hours' duration on your island off the B.C. coast. You will be in complete seclusion for this period. Apart from the usual staff of servants, major-domos, military attachés, etc., there will be nobody else except the following:

Buckingham Palace press liaison officer
Canadian Press liaison officer
   (to retain national sovereignty)
One pool reporter
One pool photographer
Two CBC-TV cameramen
Two private-TV pool cameramen

National Film Board documentary crew
Fifty-five RCMP security guards
The prime minister
George Pearkes
Blair Fraser
Honour guard
And assorted hautboys and torches

I believe that, in addition, there are several natives on the island. If you play your cards right, you might be able to talk them out of some local basket and beadwork along with the usual illuminated address, silver cigarette box, and oil painting of yourself.

They believe in doing things right in Canada, Your Royal Highness. If you take your honeymoon here, believe me we'll go all out. That is why I suggest you head for the Himalayas, or maybe the Antarctic. The weather may be rotten, but there isn't a single alderman once you pass the Great Barrier Reef.

My Country, 'Tis of Thee

TORONTO, MARCH 1—Well-known Canadian TV personality Pierre Berton announced today he is leaving Canada to start a new career in the United States.

"I have had a number of attractive nibbles from American TV, so I think it's time to make the move," Berton said.

"I want to make it very clear that I am not blaming the CBC for any of this," Berton declared. "They have done the best they can on a limited budget. It's true that they did not use my services very often, but then that is understandable when you consider the vast pool of talent available here. I have nothing but goodwill for my CBC friends and hope to return often to 'guest' on CBC programs."

Asked if he had plans to become a U.S. citizen, Berton answered with an emphatic No!

"Canada is my home," he said. "This country has been good to me. I am a Canadian first, last and always. But a talent scout caught me on *Pamela Wallin* the other night, and my agent feels I should branch out."

It is believed Mr. Berton hopes to launch his career with a guest spot on the *David Letterman Show*, giving his famous rendition of "The Shooting of Dan McGrew."

NEW YORK, OCTOBER 2—In an exclusive interview today, Pierre Berton, glamorous star of U.S. television and motion pictures, told something of the bitterness and frustration he had suffered at the hands of the Canadian Broadcasting Corporation.

He charged that the CBC "discouraged and inhibited talent," and "did not recognize true star quality." His indictment included the Canadian viewing public, which, he said, "did not believe a man had talent until he left for the United States."

Berton, whose rendition of "The Shooting of Dan McGrew" on the *David Letterman* and *Oprah Winfrey* shows skyrocketed him to almost instant stardom, told how his talents were completely neglected by the CBC for years.

"The only regular spot of any consequence that I ever had was something called *Front Page Challenge,*" Berton recalled. "The CBC gave me very little to do on this show, outside of asking a few questions of the guests, and thus I was never able to reveal my true personality. Indeed, the director tried to shape my personality completely to his own image.

"Here in the U.S. it's just the opposite. They give you your head completely."

Berton said the CBC was so niggardly with him financially that he was forced to take menial jobs such as writing "pop-history" books to make ends meet.

"Down here in the U.S.A. I find I can devote full time to my creative talents—that of reciting "The Shooting of Dan McGrew"—without any other demands on my time. It certainly wasn't that way in Canada."

Berton said it was time Canadians began to recognize native talent before it fled to greener fields.

"The trouble with the CBC," he said, "is that they refuse to institute a star system. Yet there's plenty of top people who came from there. Look at Joyce Davidson, Wayne and Shuster, Bob Goulet, Lorne Greene, René Lévesque, Laurier

Lapierre, and scores of others. They could have been big stars in their own country if people had only recognized what they had."

Berton said he had been reciting "The Shooting of Dan McGrew" at parties for years—"yet no one at the CBC understood my capabilities. That's what I mean by unrecognized talent."

He revealed that he was taking out U.S. citizenship papers and would make his home in the United States, probably in Las Vegas. "This country has been good to me," he said, "and I feel now that it is my home. It wouldn't be honest to take the money and not become an American."

In Ottawa, a CBC spokesman, commenting on Mr. Berton's charges, said that he felt the CBC had, on many occasions, provided Mr. Berton with the opportunity of demonstrating his talents but that he had not "taken full advantage of that opportunity."

Asked if the network planned to bring Mr. Berton back to Canada for a series of "specials," the spokesman said there were no present plans.

TORONTO, FEBRUARY 14—The Canadian Broadcasting Corporation announced today that it had completed contractual arrangements with Pierre Berton, noted star of stage, screen and television, for a series of six "specials" out of Toronto.

Mr. Berton, a former Torontonian and one-time casual performer on the CBC, left Canada some time ago to seek a career in the United States. He is known chiefly for his spirited rendition of "The Shooting of Dan McGrew," and it is believed that the TV shows here will all be built around that number.

"It's what he does best," a CBC spokesman said, replying to criticism that the network was again using acts previously seen here on American TV channels. "But this time we hope to give it a typically Canadian look."

Mr. Berton, contacted in Las Vegas, said he was "delighted" to appear once again "on the network that gave me my start."

"My relations with the CBC have always been cordial and I have a warm spot in my heart for them," the star said. "I think I appreciate better than most the difficulties of producing TV shows in Canada. They're doing a wonderful job up there with limited funds and limited talent, and my hat's off to them."

During his one-day visit to Toronto, where he will tape all six shows, Mr. Berton will visit the Hospital for Sick Children and appear as a guest on *Due South*. On this program he will recite "The Shooting of Dan McGrew."

Union? But What About
Our Distinctive Way of Life?

A growing number of Canadians—economists, businessmen, civic leaders, rock stars, and others—are beginning to predict that Canada's survival in the coming century lies in some sort of economic union with the United States, a union that must ultimately result in a form of political union in North America.

I have wondered if these people have thought the matter through carefully enough. Are they aware of the consequences? Do they realize that it inevitably means the destruction of our priceless Canadian heritage, the end of our distinctive national character, the finish of our unique Canadian culture, the termination of our own peculiar identity?

So that all Canadians will fully understand the implications of union with our neighbour, I have prepared a small handbook explaining the kind of thing we must be prepared for if we become Americans. This is the result of several trips to some of the better-known foreign cities beyond the border such as Buffalo, Schenectady, Niagara Falls, and Bellingham.

First let us deal with some of the more workaday aspects of American culture such as food, transportation and the like. Just as the Norman Conquest changed the eating habits of Saxon England, so the American takeover must needs change our own culinary tastes.

Americans eat "American food" and we must be prepared to follow suit. American food consists chiefly of the following staples: chow mein, pizza, pastrami, borscht, enchiladas, foot-long hot dogs, smorgasbord, sauerkraut,

French-fried potatoes, and southern-fried chicken. Canadians may find some of these items a little rich for their tastes, but visitors from the U.S.A. claim that once a liking for these dishes has been acquired they are actually quite palatable.

Americans drive "American cars," and once union is decided upon Canadians can expect to see scores of these strange automobiles in the streets. Here are the names of some typical American cars: Cadillac, Honda, Chevrolet, Volkswagen, MG, Volvo. Learn to pronounce the names and identify each car by its distinctive profile. Then you will be a real American.

As soon as U.S. political institutions take hold here, Canadians should be prepared to adopt American drinking habits. Typical American drinks include the following: bourbon, Scotch, Coca-Cola, Dr. Pepper. The most universal typical American drink, however, is Canada Dry Ginger Ale and Canadian Club. Study these drinks carefully. Ask your local bar to stock one or two of them as a goodwill gesture. Be a good neighbour.

Canadians must be prepared to accept a good many typical American sports as part of the cultural heritage that will be ours when we join the United States. Here are some American sports: hockey, baseball, golf, horse racing, gin rummy, Canadian football. It is hoped that when these sports are introduced in our country the United States will supply a small cadre of their own people to form the nucleus of local teams, since native-born Canadians are not well versed in these games.

American magazines will, of course, be featured prominently on Canadian newsstands once the two countries become one. Generally speaking, American magazines are bigger and flashier than such Canadian publications as *Maclean's, Chatelaine, Time, Reader's Digest*, etc. They do not, however, reflect the Canadian viewpoint to the same extent. Here are the names of some typical American magazines you may expect to see on your newsstand if we form a North American Common Market: *Vanity Fair, Playboy, Adam, Men's Health, Cosmopolitan, Hustler, True Medical Confessions, Teen, Superboy*, and *The New York Sunday Times*. Many of these magazines will probably be sold door to door at fantastically low prices—only a few cents a week.

American movies will, of course, quickly replace the homegrown variety and will probably become highly popular with the younger set. Here are some American movies that I have recently been privileged to see and I highly recommend: *Thank Your Lucky Stars* (Eddie Cantor and Joan Leslie); *The Big Broadcast of 1938* (Bob Hope and Shirley Ross); *Captain Blood* (Errol Flynn and Olivia de Havilland); *The Three Stooges Meet the Wolf Man*; *Think Fast, Mr. Moto* (Peter Lorre); *Charlie Chan's Greatest Case* (Warner Oland).

The same will almost certainly be true of television and we may expect at some future date that CTV and even the CBC will be carrying a goodly number of American-style TV shows. Here are the names of some typical American TV shows that we will probably be seeing once union is complete: *The X-Files*; *The Simpsons*; *Great Movies*; *America's Most Wanted*; *Melrose Place*; *Martha Stewart*; *E.R.*; and *Seinfeld*. I would guess that about half of all the programs on local stations will eventually be American and, though this

will certainly be a blow to our distinctively Canadian identity, it will, at last, allow us the opportunity of viewing such
big American name stars as Morley Safer, Peter Jennings,
Dan Aykroyd, Ivana Trump, Alex Trebek, Roger Moore,
Martin Short, Jim Carrey, and Ginger Spice.

I do not believe, however, that union with the United
States will affect our distinctively Canadian radio stations.
They, of all institutions, have their roots deep in this country
and their practice of playing the fifty most popular Canadian tunes will probably continue long after we are absorbed.

I suspect, however, that our burgeoning native theatre
will find it necessary to go international as a result of the
imbalance. I cannot see how the original purpose of the
Hummingbird Centre (né O'Keefe), for instance, as a kind
of national civic theatre can long continue once union
becomes a fact. Indeed, I suspect it may become an out-of-
town tryout house for Broadway productions or, more pos-
sibly, another whistle stop on the New York road show
circuit. I may be a bit pessimistic here.

None of this suggests, of course, that Canadians will
entirely lose their distinctive identity. I am only pointing out,
as realistically as possible, some of the pitfalls of union. Of
course, certain ruggedly Canadian traits will endure. Our
search for the Holy Grail of a Canadian identity will
undoubtedly continue unabated. *That* we will never give up!
And I continue to hew to the belief that long after we are
absorbed by the United States we will still hold searching
discussions to ask the question that forever bedevils us: What
exactly *is* a Canadian, anyway?

For Japanese Visitors:
An All-Canadian Guidebook

Those Canadians who have travelled to Japan for business or for pleasure will have read a great many books explaining the Japanese to Westerners. These books are necessary since the Japanese society is very different from that of North America or Europe. Japan has, indeed, been called "the country that does everything backwards." On the other hand, as Japan was there first, it may be we who do everything backwards. At any rate, I have written below some notes for a book that might explain those queer, backward Canadian customs to the puzzled Japanese.

MEALS

You will find Canadian meals very strange because Canadians tend to eat their meals in reverse order. It is hard to believe, but Canadians actually start their meal with soup and end with tea.

They show a great deal of manual dexterity, however, in the use of fork and knife—two implements that are absolutely essential to the meal since a great part of the preparation of the food (such as the cutting of meat, etc., into small pieces) is done right at the table and not in the kitchen.

Generally, you will find the meals somewhat monotonous, as Canadians tend to eat the same dishes all year round, and you may find it awkward to eat with Canadians since they usually serve themselves. Nonetheless, a genuine Canadian meal is one that should be experienced during your visit to the New World and you may even gain enjoyment from observing the quaint native eating customs. NOTE: Drinking liquids is done silently, as Canadians apparently do not wish to let their host know they have enjoyed anything he has served them.

BATHS

For reasons not entirely explainable, Canadians enjoy bathing in dirty water. They make no attempt to cleanse themselves before entering a bath but will jump in immediately before washing the dirt from their bodies, even getting the water murky with soap in the process.

On visiting the home of a Canadian you will rarely, if ever, be asked to bathe. Canadians appear to be ashamed of their baths. They invariably bathe in secret, and indeed all bathrooms carry locks to prevent casual entry. This has been put down to something called "modesty," but the presence of so many scantily clad people on bathing beaches, in advertisements, and on the stages of theatres and nightclubs suggests that Canadians are almost continually exposed to the contours of the nude body.

It's best for the visitor not to comment on this anomaly, however, and simply take the customs of the country as he finds them.

ATTITUDE TO MEN

The Canadian attitude toward men has been the subject of Eastern criticism and wonder for many years. There is no doubt at all that they are subjugated, though perhaps not as badly as many Japanese believe. All the same, the outward signs of subservience are quite enough to make the Japanese male travelling in Canada feel uncomfortable.

If you go into a Canadian restaurant, as a man you must expect to be served last. More than that, when accompanying any woman you must be prepared to remain two or three paces behind her. Women enter the room before a man does, and all men in that room are required by custom to stand up when any woman appears. They cannot be seated until the women take their seats.

Until very recently, when travelling in public conveyances men were also required to give up their seats to women, but this practice is going out in the post-war period as Canadian men struggle for a measure of equality.

Most decisions in Canadian households are made by women, who often go out alone to various social events leaving men to stay home and mind the house and the children. Men, on the other hand, are not usually permitted to go out by themselves for dinner, or to a nightclub (there are no geisha houses) unless accompanied by the wives, who invariably take precedence over them on such occasions.

Invitations to parties and other social affairs are almost always issued by women and accepted by women; husbands have very little to do with such things. Woman also handle the money in Canadian homes, doling out "allowances" to their menfolk.

Before we judge Canadians too harshly in this matter, it is important to understand that the men would probably not want it any other way. They are used to their submissive role in the Canadian scheme of things, and for many, no doubt, the lack of responsibility brings a tranquility of mind unknown in our Asian world.

LOVE AND MARRIAGE

The attitude to love of Canadians is very curious by Japanese standards. They harbour the odd belief—it amounts almost to an obsession—that two people can be in love without ever having lived together under the same roof or known each other intimately.

Marriages are generally based on this strange "love" concept. There is no go-between in such matters, no consideration of family: a young man will simply tell a young woman that he "loves" her; if the young woman replies that she "loves" him, the marriage then takes place in the most haphazard manner, often without recourse to the parents.

Love, in the Canadian scheme of things, does not start with marriage and grow; rather, it starts long before marriage and as often as not diminishes. A high divorce rate suggests the awkwardness of the system.

ATTITUDE TO ELDERS

Canadians by and large treat their elders in a shocking manner. Children—even those under the age of forty—frequently disobey their fathers. Married couples rarely live with their parents and if they do are treated with universal pity. Aged people are often left to fend for themselves by their children, who refuse to take them under their roof and often pop them into special homes for the aged, with which the country abounds.

Mothers-in-law are universally condemned and are the subject of many contemptuous jibes in the popular press and theatre. As a result, the government has had to initiate an elaborate scheme of old-age pensions for people who have been rejected in this manner. These are generally held to be totally inadequate, but so great is the prejudice against old people that little has been done to change their economic situation.

Three

THE HARD SELL

If Yuri Gagarin
Had Only Been a Yank!

The horrifying news that the first man into space was a Soviet astronaut certainly dealt North American show business a staggering blow. There is so little you can do with a *Russian* spaceman. Why, the fellow didn't even play the guitar.

It is becoming painfully apparent that the Russians didn't really know how to exploit Yuri Gagarin the way he'd be exploited over here. True, they held some formal press conferences and a sort of love dance in Red Square—but where, one wonders, were the signed testimonials to Crunchies? Where were the revelatory first-person, as-told-to-me-exclusively magazine articles? Where was the absolutely compulsory lecture tour of the women's clubs? Where was the ghosted advice-to-the-lovelorn column? When would the *real* Yuri Gagarin stand up on the panel show?

If Yuri had been born on this side of the water, Tin Pan Alley would already have a song on the Hit Parade about him:

He's our truest, bluest Yankee
Though he bears a foreign name,
He has struck a blow for freedom
In History's Hall of Fame. . . .
Now every true American
From Alberta to Missouri
Need have no fear!
That's why we cheer
An astronaut named Yuri!

I really missed Gagarin on the Ed Sullivan show after his triumph. One longed for the ritual interview: the tribute to Free Enterprise Initiative . . . the modest shuffling of the feet and the *Shucks, Ed, I just happened to be the guy that drew the long straw* speech . . . the surprise appearance of Yuri's childhood sweetheart, flown in through the generosity of Trans-World Airlines . . . the moving rendition of the Air Force Hymn by the 200-piece Award-Winning Band of the West Crabgrass Freedom Cadets—all capped by generous references to Yuri's forthcoming book, *Somebody Like Me Was Up There*, and a scene from the new Jerry Wald film, *The Yuri Gagarin Story*, starring Sal Mineo.

Where on earth were the Yuri dolls? Weren't the Reds hep to the promotional features of this thing? Now, if it had only been one of our boys . . . the astronaut suit in miniature could easily replace the Panda bear. Even the name is made to order: YURI. It fits a doll as easily as it fits a 72-point Franklin Gothic headline. You've got to hand it to the Russians on that score. I have an awful feeling that the Americans might have blundered and sent up somebody called Al.

The Soviets do not hold with religion, and so the customary reference to the Deity that graces the standard Hero's Speech on this side of the water was unfortunately missing. This made it just impossible for *Reader's Digest* to carry *Yuri Gagarin's Own Story*. A pity. The 15,000-word tale, planted in an obscure Javanese journal and then condensed to a few hundred gem-hard words, could have been an inspiration to millions: **A simple American farm boy tells how Faith sustained him in those awesome moments in the cosmos . . .**

Not only Faith, but other things, too, if the job had been handled by our side:

YURI GAGARIN, FIRST YANK INTO SPACE, USED BEEHIVE CORN SYRUP EXCLUSIVELY ON HIS HISTORIC FLIGHT

"Only Beehive Could Sustain Me!" Says Crack Astronaut

• • • • • •

READ HOW YURI GAGARIN, A REGULAR FELLA, KEEPS REGULAR THE BRAN-DANDY WAY!

• • • • • •

Westinghouse, Which Built the Gagarin
Space Capsule, Now Proudly Presents a
New Concept in Electric Can Openers . . .

• • • • • •

"Things were mighty tense up there for a few minutes,"
says Yuri Gagarin, a friend of Canadian Club,
"but back on good old terra firma I relaxed with . . ."

I believe I am right in saying that this was the first major adventure of modern times in which *Life* magazine did not play a leading role. Scientists had grown used to sharing bathyspheres and satellites with *Life* photographers; heiresses rarely eloped without inviting *Life* along on the honeymoon. I'm sorry *Life* missed the party; that was a real setback for our side.

Nor did we get the mandatory syndicated column that so many conquering heroes (such as Joyce Brothers) take as their due. *Yuri Gagarin's Frank Talk to Teens*? Hardly. *Yuri*

Gagarin Answers Your Questions? The answers, I fear, might be considered un-American.

The Russians did the best they could with some background human interest stories about Yuri's childhood and youth, but they really lacked the professional polish that we have come to expect in twentieth-century North America.

EXCLUSIVE!
THE DAY YURI GAGARIN TRIED SUICIDE!
Had the famed Yank astronaut taken up the piano accordion as his teacher wished, it might have meant the suicide of a notable scientific career. . . .

EXCLUSIVE!
YURI GAGARIN'S SECRET LOVE!
Only close friends know the intimate and touching story of the famed Yank astronaut's lifelong affection for the one woman responsible for his victory in space (his mother).

It is this sort of thing, I submit, that adds colour and meaning to the great achievements of our day. It is something that only the Free World seems to have mastered. The Russians may have been ahead of us in space, but when it comes to production values, good old North American know-how can't be beat.

Ten Easy Ways to
Publicize a Bank

Will the big banks join the twenty-first century? They haven't joined the twentieth. There they squat on the major intersections of every city, solid, grey edifices, pillared and porticoed, looking like something out of the Age of Pericles. It's true that there are now skyscraper bank buildings, in gold, silver and black, but they still look as forbidding as their classical counterparts. There's a gap here that ought to be filled, and if I should ever retire from the writing game, I'd like to take a whack at filling it. In short, I'd like to be a full-time public relations officer for a bank or, if those mergers go through, for THE Bank.

The thing that bothers me about banks is that they never put the merchandise in the window like other big stores. I plan to change all that. We're going to have big displays of money at street level where everybody can see it.

"*Come on in,*" the signs will read. "*Get it while it lasts!*"

And there will be a big heap of money, just asking to be borrowed.

The bank I work for will operate on a high turnover and a low mark-up, like Walmart. We are going to have specials every Tuesday. A bright new silver dollar to each of the first one hundred customers depositing more than fifty bucks between the hours of nine and eleven. Eight tellers: no waiting. Booths for ladies. And park the kids at the special playroom in the side lobby.

We will have bargain prices on interest rates. We'll suddenly announce on a Sunday night that everyone bringing in five hundred dollars before noon the following Monday will get 5 percent on his money if he'll leave it with us for twelve months.

This is the sort of slogan I intend to use:

When interest payments get ferocious
Try the Bank of Nova Scotia's!

Also, we are going to get rid of that word "teller." Instead we are going to have "hostesses," appropriately garbed. Sorry, no pimply faced "youths" or bespectacled young men need apply. We don't care about a *head* for figures—it's the figures themselves we want! They'll wear blue-and-gold satin outfits, like movie usherettes, with their first names (SYBIL, BECKY, BUBBLES, etc.) embroidered on the lapel. We'll get a lot of free publicity that way.

And on the street outside we'll have a commissionaire resplendent in epaulettes and gold braid announcing that there is absolutely no queuing at the wickets on the inside.

The advertisements, of course, will have to undergo a complete overhaul. I think we might take a leaf from the books of some of the more flamboyant loan companies. Something like this, perhaps:

Let Me Be Your Friend!

Matthew Barrett

**Ladies and gentlemen, borrowing from our bank is
downright easy. Just phone our genial "Matt" and you'll
have your money in a matter of minutes ...**

Other full-page ads might follow the principle set down
by the Toronto newspapers in comparing circulation figures.

NOW! NEWEST FIGURES PROVE
BANK OF NOVA SCOTIA LEADS
all other banks on Bay St.

	on deposit
BANK OF NOVA SCOTIA	**$127,568,342.04**
Inferior Bank "A"	**46,301,927.18**
Inferior Bank "B"	**7,010,842.01**

If one of the other banks wants to hire me I can fix this for them:

NOW! NEWEST FIGURES PROVE
CANADIAN IMPERIAL BANK OF COMMERCE
SHOWS GREATEST INCREASE IN MONEY
since last December 27.

On television I plan to use the accepted scare tech-
niques that have made this medium a must for the modern
advertiser. Security will be the theme for my dramatized
TV commercials.

WIFE: Oh, John—there's been another bank robbery down
the street. Do you suppose—?

HUBBY: No need to worry, Marcia, as long as we do business with the Bank of Montreal. Our money's always

perfectly safe in their giant coffers, thanks to new triple-tested FIBRO-MESH, the amazing new scientific vault that banishes safecrackers in an instant.

ANNOUNCER: Yes, friends—don't be half-safe. Bank with Montreal—the only bank with FIBRO-MESH!.

HUBBY: And FIBRO-MESH never affects my stomach!

Another scheme of mine is a real winner. Have you noticed that every time you go into a bank and ask to see your money, they never actually show it to you? They just show you some figures on paper.

I say this destroys confidence—the very thing I intend to build up. *Customers will actually be shown their money!* The hostess will take them to a small window, a light will flash on and there it will be—all in silver quarters in a handsome pile. Mind you, they won't be able to *get* their money, just see it. But what a sense of deep-down satisfaction it will give them.

That's what I mean about publicizing a bank. Mind you, I'm just talking off the top of my head.

How to Sell
Mail-Order Weeds

A good example of the Twentieth Century's continuing love affair with the concept of the Hard Sell can be found in the brochures and also the huge ads of the mail-order seed companies. So-called "wonder plants" guaranteed to fill your garden with armfuls of blooms turn up each spring. Actually they're the same old plants suitably disguised. Look at these examples: every word in the advertisements quoted here is true. And each picture is a faithful reproduction of the plant advertised. Actually, they are well-known weeds, every one of them. Can you guess what they are? The real names are given at the end of this piece.

NOW! From Europe comes the amazing GOLDEN CROWN . . . a flower you simply *can't be without!*
Yes, we positively guarantee that no more prolific plant exists. Once in your garden, it's yours forever. Deep-rooted and hardy, it will sustain the worst frosts or the hottest spells of a rainless summer.

Easy to grow . . . requires little cultivation . . . resists weeds. **IT WILL EVEN GROW IN TURF!** Imagine armfuls of brilliant yellow flowers suffusing your home with the aura of pure gold! Think of it—for a

small initial investment this year you can have **bushels of golden bloom** in just one, two or three seasons because GOLDEN CROWN multiplies by itself! No need to buy expensive replacements . . .

. . . Thanks to this amazing zinnia-like plant you can have **fields of flowers for only a few cents!**

Yes, that's right . . . Imagine a sheet of solid yellow brightening your driveway next May. You'll be the envy of the neighbours if you buy GOLDEN CROWN . . .

Special offer for one week, 6 plants . . . . . . only $5.62

* * *

THE INCREDIBLE SNOWSTORM PLANT!
Now at Bargain Rates!

You don't want to be without this fantastic novelty—a delight for children and adults and an asset to any garden . . . Known in ancient Greece, where it was called *asclepias*, the **SNOWSTORM PLANT** is now available here in limited quantities . . . One of the few flowering perennials that **actually imitates an actual snowstorm.**

Yes, unbelievable as it sounds, this Snowstorm Plant sends *blizzards of white bloom* causing children to squeal with delight. Yet it also produces gigantic lilac-coloured flowers—each one a slightly different hue.

No other plant like it. Don't disappoint your child.
Be the first in your neighbourhood to own and grow
a plant that everybody's talking about.
6 plants . . . . . . only $3.

* * *

WHO ELSE WANTS A GARDEN OF PALE GREEN AND GLITTERING PINK?

That's what you'll have when you plant **PINK MAGIC,** the incredible new plant imported from the wilds of continental Asia. A close relative of the forget-me-not, **PINK MAGIC** actually grows much taller while its delicate flowers are pure magenta pink. The Chinese have known about this plant for years. Now it can be yours, too, for a fraction of the original cost, absolutely guaranteed against frost, drought, or garden pests. *Yes, that's right! We guarantee that PINK MAGIC cannot be killed by normal garden conditions, that it can even grow in subsoil, even in thick weeds.* Imagine owning a flower you don't have to weed and that **seeds** itself **year after year** without further expense or trouble to you. **And it blooms all summer . . .**

But that's not all: Pink Magic's soft grey-green foliage will delight you. The unique velvet leaves provide a background that will make you the envy of the neighbourhood.
Order your PINK MAGIC plants while they last.
8 plants . . . . only $4.23

* * *

AT LAST! A Perennial flower that grows MAN SIZE in just two months!

Yes, we know it's hard to believe, but when you get your amazing new **SKYSCRAPER PLANT** you'll discover that *miracles can happen!*

Think of it! A flower that can grow as high as six feet in a single summer and produce masses of lemon-yellow blooms on spikes **as long as three feet! And these giant spikes of flowers last—not just for days—but for weeks!**

Can you imagine the oohs! and aahs! of your friends when they see one of these luxurious giant Skyscraper Plants lofting above your home? And can you imagine the envy with which they'll greet a vase topped by one of these incredible mammoth flowers?

Easy to grow, these luxurious Mediterranean plants come absolutely guaranteed to withstand the Canadian winter. But act quickly to avoid disappointment.
2 plants . . . . only \$5.75.

* * *

**Now from the mountain fastness of Eurasia
comes a flower as delicate as a lace doily!**

ABSOLUTELY UNIQUE these enormous flowers seem
to have been crocheted by hand by a master lacemaker!

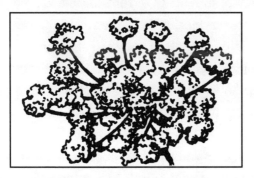

Often half a foot across, these gigantic blooms will thrill you
both in the garden and in the home because **there is no other
flower in the world quite like them!** *Borne on sturdy
stalks, growing as high as a school-age child, delicately
fashioned blooms last and last and last . . .*

Just imagine your perennial border in July and August dominated by these **unbelievable saucer-size blossoms** that will
come back, year after year, requiring little or no care to make
your home a showplace.

**From the steppes of Central Asia
to your garden for only $1.98.**

* * *

1. Dandelion   **2.** Milkweed
3. Hounds tongue *(Common burr)*
4. Great mullein   **5.** Queen Anne's lace

Smart Funerals
for Smart People

You've got to hand it to the funeral business: it's come a long way in our past century—from the plain pine box to the stainless steel cryptorium with the solid-bottom, 100-percent non-imbedding base. By George, that's progress.

The undertakers are moving with the times. Just the other day I was shown an advertising brochure sent out by one of them to old people's picnics. Here, surely, is free enterprise in action!

And yet, one wonders, has the funeral industry fully realized its enormous potential? I think not. What is needed, surely, is a more aggressive public relations campaign to push the idea of Smart Funerals for Smart People.

At the risk of sticking my nose into other people's business, I have some modest suggestions to offer the industry to help push sales in the century to come.

I do not mean inconspicuous slogans tucked away in newspaper ads. *"None of Our Customers Ever Kicked Yet!"* That sort of thing belongs to the past. I urge the funeral people to Think Big.

The main thing we have to do, men, is to convince the public that it pays to order an expensive funeral. After all, it is a long-term investment. More than that, it pays in prestige (the smart, sociable set ought to be putty in our hands) and in *"Peace-of-Mind."*

I don't quite know what the last phrase means, but it has a nice oily ring to it and I offer it free. A pamphlet put out, say, by a manufacturer of burial vaults might read like this:

THE ULTIMATE IN
PEACE-OF-MIND PROTECTION:

**After the hymns are still . . .
the fond words softy spoken . . .
the living find quiet comfort in the
knowledge that the ultimate in care
and affection has been accorded
their loved one . . .**

**Many national leaders and well-known
people have been interred in the respected
Wilbert Burial Vaults. The scientifically
engineered combination of quality-controlled,
special pre-cast asphalt faced with
quality-controlled reinforced
concrete provides the maximum
of peace-of-mind protection . . .**

The idea we want to push is that when you're encased in one of these vaults you never actually die.

We must go a step further, however. The idea of the funeral as a Status Symbol should be engrained in the customers' minds from earliest childhood. I have prepared the following set of crude drawings suitable for inclusion in comic books, Boy Scout manuals, etc.

I wonder, too, if the idea of the *cheap* funeral as a Low Status Symbol can't be implanted by subtle advertising such as this:

SPECIAL! WHILE THEY LAST!
PAUPERS' FUNERALS
ONLY $250

This should fix it so nobody will dare spend that little when committing Aunt Lottie to the clay.

In this connection, the advantages of daytime radio advertising should not be neglected. The following brief recorded dialogue could well form the basis for an appealing commercial message:

JULIA: Why so cheerful, Marcia?

MARCIA: I've just come from the funeral parlour, Julia, selecting a casket for mother; and I just wish you could see the stunning model we've picked out: It's a Connersville-Franklin Casket of Distinction, you know, and the Log Mould Style Shell has all the majestic beauty . . . all the peace and grandeur of solid oak. And what's more, the exclusive Protecto-coating resists marring and corrosion. No other casket has it!

JULIA: Gee, Marcia, wait till I tell the girls at the bridge club. How envious they're going to be!

QUARTET SINGS:

If you're headed for extinction,
> **Reached the End of the Road:**
Get a Casket of Distinction
> **And you'll never corrode!**

Another scheme, which I am sure the funeral directors will welcome, is to convince social editors that funerals, like weddings, ought to be reported in detail. I mean, why waste all that Grey Mist Cheney Velvet interior lining if nobody is going to notice?

BREATHTAKING COLOUR DESIGN
FEATURES HARVEY GREBE RITES

Exotic pastel shades, sparked by accents of bright indigos and carmines, marked the last rites of Harvey J. Grebe, socially prominent businessman, at the McGhoul and Creep Slumber Room.

Attired in a specially tailored blue business suit with matching tie (by Kellow Burial Wear), Mr. Grebe was laid to rest in a solid bronze casket by Merit, with the Blond Heather Rose Rubbed Finish. For the interior decor, Mrs. Grebe chose mauve crêpe de Chine.

The final drive to the fashionable Garden of Peace was made in a spanking new Crown Victoria Landaulet with Criterion Styling.

Mind you, fellows, this is just me talking. . . .

Remember the
Thinking Man's Filter?

The Hard Sell's greatest triumph in the Twentieth Century was the long campaign of the tobacco companies to convince us all that *cigarette smoking was good for us.* In the face of incontrovertible evidence, they soldiered on. Only recently, with advertising curtailed and tobacco taxes rising, have they suffered a setback.

But who can forget the glory days when everybody from Ed Murrow to Humphrey Bogart was a walking advertisement for the weed? Who can forget the Great Filter-Trap Race? Its crowning achievement was the introduction, by Viceroy Cigarettes, of the Thinking Man's filter. Someday a plaque will be erected in Winston-Salem, North Carolina, to the unknown adman who conceived the idea and brought it full blown to the TV networks.

Take, for instance, the series of inspiring vignettes that dominated our small screens during those far-off days. In one of them, for example, we were introduced to a rough creature at work building a brick wall.

"Ah," says the announcer, "a bricklayer?"

"Certainly not!" says the rough creature. "I happen to be the conductor of a famous symphony orchestra in one of our leading cities."

Why then is he laying bricks? Because he is a Thinking Man and because he smokes Viceroy cigarettes, which contain a Thinking Man's filter but have a Smoking Man's taste.

Apparently, Viceroy had scoured the country for Thinking

Men: plumbers who painted abstract pictures, salesmen who played the drums, prominent bankers who dug ditches, skilled cracksmen who were mad about petit point.

I once turned on my TV set, for instance, and was truly delighted by the following scene. We were treated to a view of an elegant nightclub: men in faultless evening dress, women in bejewelled gowns, an enormous orchestra, waiters floating about with carafes of this and magnums of that, and in the foreground two impeccably groomed young people indulging in small talk.

"What is it that Viceroy gives to you that makes the flavour grand?" the girl asked casually, proving once and for all that the art of conversation is not dead.

"Twice as many of these filter traps as any other brand," the boy replied gaily. And he held up a Viceroy that was positively bulging with filter traps.

That, of course, was the first winter of the Great Filter-Trap Race, an event almost totally neglected by the boys on the sports pages although it was as exciting a contest as any we've seen since the Bufferin people discovered that famous stomach valve.

You may recall that when the lung cancer scare began and the tobacco people found it politic to replace cork tips with filters, your average filter contained, oh, not more than ten thousand filter traps, give or take twenty-five. I mean, that was common knowledge at the time.

But then Viceroy, in a truly awesome display of technical know-how, produced a filter that contained twenty-thousand tiny filter traps. And in a brilliant coup, they hired Rex

Marshall, the most believable TV announcer of that day, to get their scoop across to the public.

Marshall had made his name touting millions of tiny flavour buds for Maxwell House, and it was a piece of cake for him to switch his pitch to thousands of tiny filter traps.

Not to be outdone, however, another company, working on a crash program that must have made the Manhattan Project seem like the Schomberg Strawberry Festival, produced a filter that contained *thirty* thousand filter traps.

Now we get a glimpse of the kind of all-out teamwork that got *Explorer* halfway to the moon. Within weeks, it seemed, somebody (I forget who, now) had a cigarette on the market that contained *one hundred* thousand filter traps!

Viceroy promptly dropped out of the filter-trap race and invented the Thinking Man. Rex Marshall was put out to pasture and when last seen was standing in front of a chart talking about millions of tiny microbes. I fear he was badly typed.

By now the filter situation had become incredibly confused. We not only had the Thinking Man but we also had the Thoughtful Man. He turned up on TV on Sunday.

You had to be a student of the cigarette commercials to understand the significance of this.

First, you had to understand that filter cigarettes were trying to suggest that (*a*) cigarettes with no filters were harmful and (*b*) other brands of filter cigarettes were downright sinister. For instance, the new Hi-Fi Parliament, which was a cigarette and not a record album, was touted as containing No Filter Feedback. The suggestion seemed to be that other filters sort of hurled the nicotines and tars back into your mouth in a poisonous shower.

Second, you had to believe that cigarettes with no filters were somehow sneaky and underhand. "No filter, no foolin'," Mike Wallace used to say earnestly about Philip Morris, before he began to plug filters. And Lucky Strike took to talking about the "honest taste of fine tobacco." That was a nice ploy. After all, who wants to be called a crook?

Pall Mall was trying to get the best of both worlds. It was being sold to Thoughtful Men as a filter cigarette without a filter. It was extra long, see, and the *tobacco itself* acted like a filter. This meant you could Light Both Ends, if you didn't mind burning your mouth.

And the filter-trap race? It went on and on until smokers began to realize they were being conned. Before it was over, however, the news burst upon us that Hit Parade cigarettes had broken the sound barrier: 400,000 filter traps! No honest taste, maybe, like Lucky Strikes, which were made by the same firm. But 400,000—that's close to half a million! The mind boggles. The imagination reels.

The Hard Sell, as we know it today, did not exist in the early years of the Twentieth Century. Consider, for instance, the advertisements that appeared in *The Canadian Countryman* in the years following the Great War. How ancient they seem today with their quiet prose and their soft approach. How would a modern advertising man rephrase some of these muted appeals? Here are some examples. The original ads are printed just as they were written in those far-off days. Suggestions for a new, up-to-date version follow each example.

• • • • • •

(Original ad: 1918)
Don't be endlessly changing needles
Buy a Pathéphone and enjoy your records

Not only do the old-time steel needles mar your full enjoyment of the
music you play on your phonograph, but they injure your favourite
records. The Pathéphone plays with
a permanent genuine Sapphire Ball,
smooth and highly polished, which
does away with the everlasting
bother of changing needles. It cannot scratch or wear records, and will
play not one or two but literally
thousands of Pathé Records without
the slightest wear.

If you are planning to buy a phonograph, you should certainly hear the Pathéphone. You will be enchanted by its wonderful tone. If you already have a phonograph, it can be easily equipped to play Pathé records—or, better still, any Pathé agent will make a liberal allowance for it in exchange for one of the new Pathéphones, which plays any record.

(Modern version, with picture of pretty housewife)

"Won't the girls at the bridge club be envious when they hear we've got a Pathéphone with the new LIFE-TIME JEWEL NEEDLE!"

"Bill wanted me to have the best, even though it was slightly more expensive, that's why he chose Pathéphone, the phonograph that *positively does away with steel needles.*"

Yes, that's the really fantastic thing about Pathéphone. Thanks to an amazing new scientific discovery, tested for eight years in Pathé's giant research laboratories, Pathéphone has developed a new LIFETIME needle, made of solid, genuine Sapphire—a needle that plays not just once, not just twice, but *for the actual life* of the phonograph itself!

Think of it! You actually play thousands of records and never change the needle! No messy twisting of wing nuts, no dangerous cuts from handling old needles, no moving parts to get broken—just a simple flick and it's there for life.

And Pathéphone is so easy to play, too . . . a child can handle it! Just turn the crank, slip on the record, adjust the genuine sapphire Lifetime needle in the groove and the music of the masters is at your fingertips.

For those who demand the finest—it's Pathéphone.

• • • • • •

(Original ad: 1925)
NO PIE CAN BE BETTER THAN ITS CRUST

If your pie-crust isn't always what you would like it to be, don't blame the recipe, or the oven—chances are it's the flour that's wrong. Purity Flour, milled from the finest hard wheat, silk-sifted and oven tested is fully worthy of your talent for baking. With Purity Flour you can always make flaky, golden-brown, delicious-tasting piecrust.

(Modern version, with picture of pie)

Bake This Fabulous HOLLYWOOD PIE with the Flour the Stars Use!!!

You can hardly drag Francis X. Bushman and Lillian Gish out of their kitchens these days because they've switched to *Purity*, the new, easy, all-purpose flour that banishes bake-day blues and turns kitchen drudgery into exhilarating fun!

If you've been dreading bake-days, then here's fabulous news for you—news about an amazing new oven-tested flour that in the *twinkling of an instant* produces pies that will make you the envy of your neighbourhood.

Yes, that's right. Unbelievable as it sounds, Purity is fantastically simple to use: Just add flour, lard, salt, water and stir, mix and roll out and bake to a golden brown. Lovely Mae Marsh says: "Since I switched to Purity I've been able to devote precious hours to my books, music and china painting."

. . . and remember:
Purity is "Silk-Sifted"

● ● ● ● ● ●

(Original ad: 1925)

**Choose your Christmas Radio from
among the Famous Rogers Receiving Sets.
Investigate the "Rogers"
Now and Learn Why These Sets
Have Won Such Popularity.**

Rogers Radio Receiving Sets are designed by leading Radio
Engineers and built under their skilled technical supervision.
These powerful sets will bring to your home the Continent's
best programs with a tone volume and clarity rarely found in
sets of their size. Plan now for the enjoyment of Radio "as it
should be" in your home this Christmas and during the coming long winter evenings.

(Modern version, with picture of unhappy family)

"It's Christmas—But Santa Forgot the "Rogers"

Every family in the block has a Rogers Radio—except the
Joneses. Santa forgot this family and Dad's mighty blue
about it.

What's Christmas without a radio blaring in the front
room—in every room. Don't be a piker this Yuletide. Get
every member of your family a Rogers two-tube radio receiving set!

Make every day Christmas Day—with Rogers!

• • • • • •

(Original ad: 1925)

COZY FLOORS FOR INDOOR DAYS

There is nothing like cheerful, colourful Dominion Linoleum for brightening up every room in the house and making such an improvement that everyone will notice it. And such wonderful wear—nothing seems to hurt the  firm, smooth, weatherproof surface of Dominion Linoleum . . .

(Modern version)

That "Model Home" Look with Dominion Linoleum
The *wall-to-wall flooring that fits all budgets!*

When it comes time to clean *this* floor, "Mummy" can stop running. A blob of paste, crushed chalk, a sticky crayon—a bit of a wipe with a damp cloth and they're gone. Dominion Linoleum resists it marvellously. But if scratches *do* appear (and with toys . . . *you* know!) the pattern makes them practically invisible.

Price? Surprisingly reasonable—even more so when you install Dominion Linoleum yourself. And it takes *wear* like a teddy bear, so replacement costs are nil . . .

I have to confess that this last example of a rewritten ad is not an invention. It was taken, word for word, from an issue of *Canadian Homes and Gardens* more than thirty years after the original. Nice to see Dominion Linoleum moving with the times.

Four

MORE FABLES
FROM OUR TIME

Everyone Truly
a Hostess

The following pamphlet, which was once distributed to customers of the Embers Dining Room in the now defunct
Prince George Hotel in Toronto, is expected to be one of several exhibits in the forthcoming "Anthology of Twentieth-
Century Absurdities" now being assembled by students in
the Social History 101 class, University of Calgary.

**In most restaurants the responsibility for pleasant dining
finally comes to rest on the "waitress." She is the one who
can really make a guest feel at home—welcome, wanted.
Only she can create the genuine atmosphere of friendliness and hospitality. Her personality and attitude will
either bring him back for another meal or send him away
for good with burping indigestion.**

**The good "waitress" is wife, mother, hostess, salesla-
dy and "public relations agent" all in one. She must be a
happy person herself, she must like people. She must be
service-minded. She must have highly developed social
skills—"plain good manners," if you please. Her personality must emanate charm, friendliness and genuine desire
to please. She must have a high degree of selflessness.**

**Now for heaven's sake let's not call a lady like that a
"waitress"—she's a real HOSTESS in every sense of the
word.**

**Therefore we no longer have waitresses—each and
every lady in our employ is truly a HOSTESS.**

• • • • • •

What was it about this Toronto dining room that set it apart from all the others? Today, it stands out as a kind of beacon illuminating the otherwise drab atmosphere of early Hogtown gastronomy. Have things deteriorated since the time when young women were encouraged to acquire certain skills before daring to proffer so much as a wine list? Perhaps the following fable—based on a true story, as the movie people always say—may serve to illuminate the situation.

ALICIA VAN NOSTRAND, girl hostess, reluctantly put down her copy of Kierkegaard's *Philosophical Fragments* and prepared to start her day. Examining herself in the mirror now, her persimmon-coloured hair framing her sensitive face, she was not displeased at what she saw. Wife, mother, saleslady, public relations agent and all-round troubleshooter for Toronto's sveltest dining spot, she had still retained that haunting beauty, friendliness and genuine desire to please that caused patrons of the famed Prince Gustav Hotel to storm the doors of its Cinders Room nightly.

She ran a slim, vermilion-tipped finger down her appointment pad: 10:00 a.m. her lecture in Social Skills at the U. of T.; 11:00 a.m., sales meeting with the staff; 12:00, business luncheon with several brewery tycoons who wanted her to head up the United Way Campaign; 2:00 p.m., a cocktail party for the press to announce the hiring of a new busboy; 4:30 p.m., visit to Sunnybrook where she regularly mothered several veterans whose past patronage of the Prince Gustav had made them eligible for pension. Then dinner at the Cinders Room and perhaps, if there was time, a "trick" at waiting on tables.

But first, she must attack her voluminous correspondence. Fifty letters awaited her, each seeking her wifely advice, her motherly counsel, each appealing to her high degree of selflessness.

DEAR AUNT ALICIA:

For seven wonderful months I have been going with this girl—the sweetest creature to tread God's earth. Yet now she seems vaguely cool. When I rap on her door she grabs the chocolates, talks about having a headache and shuts me out. I try to tell her if she'll get rid of the stale cigar smoke in her flat, it might clear up the migraine, but she will have none of it. What should I do?
—BEWILDERED.

To which Alicia replied in her best Ann Landers style:

DEAR BEWILDERED:

How square can you get, lover boy? The cigar smoke isn't Chanel and if you were dry behind the ears you'd know the gate when you see it. Wise up: you're through . . .

Then she bethought her public relations duties and added:

Meanwhile, there's nothing like a real home-style dinner to take your mind off your troubles. So why not drop into the famed Cinders Room today and try one of their chef's specials:

plump, tiny, bite-sized *médaillions* of Grade A filet that melt in your mouth, cooked to your order and steeped in our secret marinade (a subtle blend of tarragon, peach brandy, and grape leaves), the whole swimming in rich, creamery country-fresh butter and topped with calorie-free whipped cream, brought to you on a sizzling platter with a generous side order of oven-crisp onion rings and a genuine, jumbo-size Prince Edward Island baked potato topped with chopped chives, sour cream, bacon, and anchovies: yours for a paltry $1.97.

—Yours,

AUNT ALICIA

Her secretary slid into the office.

"Mr. Carrington called three times, Madame. He seemed impatient."

Alicia coloured. Philip Armbruster Carrington III, scion of an immense fortune, had eyes only for her. Dear Philip! She *was* fond of him, but work must come first! And yet, a small voice whispered, if it wasn't for her high degree of self-lessness perhaps she and Philip . . . But why torture herself? She could be wife only to the customers of the groaning boards of the Prince Gustav.

It was late that evening when Alicia Van Nostrand final-ly reached the Cinders Room. Her appointments had been running behind all day and now, as Anthrax Vestibule, the general manager, met her, she foresaw more problems.

"Miss Van Nostrand! You are late again and the guests are restive. There is no one to serve old Mr. Shrevnitz, our most faithful patron. At 2 p.m. he ordered one of our country-fresh

mouth-melting peach strudels smothered with Special Formula sour cream and topped with delicately shaved chocolate chips. It's 8:30 and he still hasn't got it."

"Poor dear," murmured Alicia, "he wants mothering."

"Not so," replied the other. "He wants his strudel. Please,
Alicia, couldn't you just this once—"

"Serve table?" cried Alicia. "That's what you're getting
at, isn't it? And me with a board meeting in half an hour.
Why, you people aren't human!"

Then suddenly the cloud vanished from her lovely face
as a thought struck her.

"I think I have the solution!" she exclaimed. "Don't tell
me Alicia Van Nostrand hasn't got her ear down where the
rubber meets the road! Mind you, I'm just blowing smoke
rings—but why don't we hire us some plain, ordinary girls:
simple creatures with nothing more than a senior matric
background and Latin options? We pay them peanuts, fit
them into black-and-white uniforms with "Sally" embroidered on the pockets, teach them to spill coffee, and let them
sling hash eight hours a day. Am I orbiting, A.V.?"

"It's plain genius!" Anthrax cried. "It'll revolutionize the
restaurant business! But wait: we've got to have a name for
these—these persons."

Alicia knitted her brows.

"Look," she said finally. "It's kind of corny, I know, but—
how about calling them 'waitresses'? I mean, it has a certain
dignity and yet it hits the common people where they live."

"It's sheer poetry," cried the general manager.

P.S.: They lived happily ever after.

Raven van Lure's
Mysterious Past

The story of the meteoric rise of Raven van Lure, the glamorous Hollywood actress, is too well known to bear repeating here. She made her name, you will remember, playing the real-life story of another glamorous Hollywood actress, Angela Carp, a girl unfortunately addicted to hashish. This frank and revealing screen document won for Raven an Academy Award nomination.

Later—and this is, of course, ancient history now—Raven scored another smash hit in the real-life story of Gladys del Shriv, the blonde bombshell of Hollywood, whose tragic addiction to Cream Soda, bared in all its sordid details, made her a mint of money and won, for Raven, the PREMIERE award as actress of the month.

It was after Raven zoomed to stardom playing the real-life story of Adele Morowitz, girl wrestler (whose unhappy love affair with a Siamese twin became a Book-of-the-Month Club Dividend), that her agent, Manny O'Hoolihan, decided something ought to be done.

"Raven-doll," said Manny, "it's time you wrote your own real-life story, hiding nothing, baring everything. It's time you, too, were Startlingly Frank. We got to get in on the gravy, kid."

"Anything you say, Manny," Raven told him, lacquering her nails a delicate powder blue after the fashion of the day. "You are the doctor, Manny."

"The way I see it, Raven-doll," said Manny O'Hoolihan,

"the way I see it, this one can't lose. This one will be really big. Because we got something going for us the others didn't have. In spite of your sordid background, in spite of your tragic and unbelievable past, in spite of the terrible privations you've suffered and the weaknesses of the flesh to which you have succumbed—in spite of all this you still have that fresh, untouched look. That is why you were chosen to play the parts of Angela Carp, hashish smoker, Gladys del Shriv, Cream Soda addict, and Adele Morowitz, slave to a Siamese twin."

"Sure, Manny," said Raven, adjusting her luxurious knee-length stole of mutant vicuna. "Sure, Manny."

"And so," cried Manny O'Hoolihan, press agent extraordinaire, "and so you, Raven van Lure, *will play yourself* in the screen version of your best-selling, revealingly frank, ghosted autobiography, *Too Late to Die*!

"Why," burbled Manny O'Hoolihan, "the very novelty of it will shake Hollywood to its foundations and bring the customers through the turnstiles in waves! It's an Oscar for sure, Raven baby-doll."

"Whatever you say, Manny," said Raven, as she stepped into her all-lavender Jaguar with the turquoise wheels. "You set it up, Manny."

Thus, it came about that a few days later Egbert Frayne, the famous Hollywood ghost writer and anonymous author of such raging best-sellers as *I Had It Bad* (Diane Larose); *Up from the Slime* (Lucille Balchance) and *Too Much, Too Often* (Julia L'Amethyste), knocked on Raven van Lure's door.

For almost ten years Egbert Frayne had been practising

the difficult art of getting hysterical, overwrought movie actresses to talk frankly about their Past. After that, Frayne thought to himself glumly, he had had to practise the even more difficult art of getting them to shut up.

And it was an art! he told himself proudly as he pressed the tiny cultured-pearl button that rang the chimes in Raven's flat. To take the incoherent ramblings of an ex-drunk and render them into sympathetic prose was artistry of the highest order. You could babble all you liked about Hemingway and Faulkner; the guy who really deserved the Nobel Prize was Egbert Frayne!

Now, seated beside Raven van Lure on the albino yak's hair settee, Frayne once again assumed the softly insinuating tones that had rung confessions from women who would normally have remained obdurate under the hot lights of a Red inquisition.

"Just let it pour out naturally, Miss van Lure. Hold nothing back. Tell all. Remember that I, Egbert Frayne, am your friend."

"Sure, Egbert," said Raven. "Whatya wanna know?"

This is going to be easier than I thought, thought Egbert: a breeze.

"Tell about your terrible struggles with The Bottle," he said encouragingly.

"You bet," said Raven. "What bottle?"

"Whisky," said Egbert. "Demon rum. Tell how you leaned on it as a crutch when your second love affair broke wide open and you felt that life meant nothing."

"Oh," said Raven shrilly. "*Liquor!* But I don't drink; it's something that simply isn't allowed for one single moment in the Church of the Little Father!"

For a second, Egbert Frayne was nonplussed. The Church of the Little Father! This was a new twist. But maybe a religious angle made it better . . .

"Those marks on your arm," he said, and his voice was as smooth as a giant triple-whipped supersonic chocolate malted. "Poor child, how you must have suffered from the needle! And all because you were secretly in love with your father. Tell me how you kicked the habit. Was it the turning point in your career?"

Raven looked curiously at the object of Frayne's interest.

"That's my vaccination," she said. "My folks was against it, being antivivisectionists, but the studio insisted."

Frayne felt a little weak, but still game.

"Your first wild love affair," he said. "Give me all the details."

"I've only had one," said Raven dubiously.

"Just one shattering affair—and then blackness!" cried Frayne, exalted. "And so you sought solace in your career and in Other Things."

"It wasn't so much," said Raven. "Just one little kiss with Arnie Flamheaver in the vestry. I didn't like him much, and what with choir work and all the mission school I just haven't had time for boys, really."

"Just one little kiss," murmured Egbert Frayne "mission school . . ." His knees turned to rubber and a sob escaped him as he groped blindly for the door. Raven van Lure never saw him again.

Perhaps it is mere coincidence, but her decline in the film world seems to have begun almost at that moment. Today she is nothing more than a name in an old fan magazine, a footprint in the worn cement of Grauman's Chinese, a haunted face on the Late Show.

But in the Church of the Little Father, she is as big a draw as ever.

The Legend of
Healing Mountain

Once upon a time, a long time ago, in another part of the country, there was a small but serviceable mountain.

The Indians called it Healing Mountain because there were hot springs on its flanks from which healing waters spouted—or so the medicine men said.

Sometimes smoke came out of the top of the mountain, and the Indians said there was a Spirit inside; and because they were afraid of this Spirit they were Good Indians.

This made it very easy for the white men to steal the mountain and build a hotel at its base and pipe the waters into the main lobby and send out coloured brochures about it.

So the town of Healing Mountain began to boom, thanks to the chamber of commerce whose membership was made up entirely of real estate men, hotel owners, and nightclub managers.

They fixed it so you could get anything you wanted in Healing Mountain.

You could get devil dogs, salami-burgers, super orange drinks, quadruple-decker club sandwiches with two kinds of cream cheese plus bacon and chicken, giant foot-long pizzas, shrimp chips by the bushel, southern-fried larks' tongues to take out, nectar and ambrosia ice-cold to go.

You could get crying drunk in Cheerful Charlie's Paradise Bar, Fred's Gay Room, Jack's Happy Joint, Herbie's Laff Lounge, Hank's Fun Place, or Ned's Joy Room We Never Close.

You could get a divorce in ten days without cause or get married in ten minutes without questions.

The dog-tracks ran all day and the casinos ran all night, and there was a slot machine in every drugstore and a bingo game in every church basement.

And, since 10 percent of the net proceeds after taxes were donated entirely to charity, everybody felt good about it.

The main street was called The Platinum Strip, and it had the biggest motels in the world, the biggest saloons in the world, and the biggest casinos.

And it had souvenir shops selling bottles of healing water and Genuine Indian souvenirs made in eastern factories by Genuine Indians, and restaurants constructed entirely of glass featuring foot-thick abalone steaks and Zombies one to a customer.

And it had a Drive-In Divorce Court and a Drive-In Roulette Wheel and a Drive-In Psychoanalyst and a Drive-In Church so you never had to get out of your car or go down on your knees for any occasion.

Healing Mountain was Cadillactown and Swimming Poolville and Mink City where Health Can Be Fun, especially if you put a shot of vodka in the sulphur water.

Healing Mountain was the Fun Capital of North America, and everybody who was anybody and everybody who was nobody visited it.

The town council was crooked and everybody knew it and nobody cared.

The wheels were all fixed and everybody knew it and nobody cared.

The schools were falling apart and everybody could see that, but nobody gave it a thought.

Nobody had time because everybody was too busy Having Fun.

Preachin' Jack Carstairs, the great evangelist, came to town and held a Drive-In Revival Meeting, and thousands flocked to hear the message of the Lord.

Preachin' Jack cried out that Healing Mountain was more wicked than Pompeii of old, and when he began to tell in detail how wicked Pompeii was, the faithful turned the speakers up in their ears so as not to miss a word.

Scores drove their Cadillacs right down to the jewelled dais where Preachin' Jack was calling down the wrath of God, and they declared themselves for Christ, right there and then, without turning off the ignition.

There was a new sensation the following week when a famous seismologist announced that the pressure within the mountain was greater than the pressure without.

Everybody had fun with that one.

The nightclub comics made jokes about the pressures of modern living, and Cheerful Charlie's bar featured a Healing Mountain Pressurized Special guaranteed to blow your head off, and the newspapers got an Indian to say the great spirit in the mountain was heap angry.

And everybody said that if the mountain was going to blow up there was nothing much they could do about it, so they might as well have fun.

That week they opened a new Drive-In swimming pool complete with klieg lights, Hollywood stars, and free orchids to the first hundred women.

The next week Healing Mountain blew up.

It blew with a bang, sending a sinister cloud a mile high, which, on descent, covered the town with seven and one-half feet of hot ash.

After that a torrent of boiling lava poured down the mountainside and covered the ash with a foot-thick skin of molten rock.

And everything was covered, including six new, restricted subdivisions, only recently completed, and the Drive-In racetrack on the outskirts.

And nothing was left, save a few frayed posters plugging the preacher's talks on Pompeii and a handful of old Popsicle wrappers drifting south on the wings of a hot, dry wind, and the mountain itself, which, having accomplished its healing work, slept peacefully as of old.

Angela Nostrum, girl heiress, sat disconsolately on the edge of the chaise longue, waiting—as she had waited now for thirty-six hours—for the phone to ring.

If only Reginald deBryce Faversham would call; perhaps then they could pick up the shattered remnants of their lives!

All that was needed was for Reggie to make the first gesture: the tiny, conciliatory movement of dialing her number, and she would forgive anything. For she needed Reggie deBryce Faversham—needed him desperately with a hunger passing comprehension.

Outside, the rain beat its leaden tattoo on the leaded panes of her window. Somewhere, in the far distance, a lark sang. There were other sounds, too: a train whistle, lonely as a cry in the night; several church bells; two or three bursts of gunfire; and the usual sounds of automobiles smashing together at the intersection below. Angela was oblivious to them all. She was waiting for the phone to ring.

Then suddenly she knew it would never ring again. She was calm now, for she understood what she must do. From the drawer of her desk she drew a small revolver and slipped it into her purse. The moonlight glinted, as it usually does in such cases, on the blue steel.

Angela stood up, only the chalk white of her cheeks betraying her inner emotions, and strode resolutely to the door.

Her hand was on the catch when suddenly, like an explosion

in that quiet room, there came the insistent ringing of the phone.

She stood stock still. It was too late! She would not answer it. And yet . . . .and yet . . . Suddenly Angela Nostrum was back on the chaise longue, tears of relief streaming down her cheeks, as with trembling hands she lifted the receiver to hear the familiar voice on the other end of the line.

"Reggie! Reggie! It's you! You *did* call!"

"It's not Reggie," said the familiar voice. "This is radio station CHOO. And we're going to give you fifty silver dollars if you can identify the Hit Song of the Week!"

• • • • • •

Alfie Snitch, boy spiv, paced the linoleum of his incredibly shoddy East London flat, beads of perspiration glistening on his goose bumps.

He had exactly seven and one-half minutes left to raise 5,000 quid. If he didn't pay up *They* would get him. Alfie shivered in spite of the unseasonably hot gaslight that played upon his sallow face. When you dealt with Gristle Make-fast, King of the Bookmakers, you paid your debts on the button—or else!

But how was Alfie to know that Sibling Rivalry, as pretty a filly as ever took goof pills, would snap a fetlock on the first corner and breathe her last in the mud of Epsom?

And now he had 5,000 quid to raise by 6 p.m., and it all depended on whether or not his pal, Lester, could fence that last shipment of hot spices from fabled Cathay before the deadline.

If only Lester would call! And Alfie looked again at the

telephone, which, together with a kitchen chair, was the only object of furniture in the room. He tried to will it to ring—but there was only silence.

The insistent ticking of the clock now filled the room, hammering into Alfie's brain like a bullet. The minute hand was almost closing over the numeral when Alfie heard the heavy tread on the stair.

A moment later, framed in the doorway, he could see the bullet heads of two enormous men.

"We've come from Gristle Makefast," they growled, and Alfie could see the moonlight glinting on the blue steel of a straight razor.

At that instant the phone rang, and Alfie sprang to it with a squeal of relief. On the other end of the line he could hear a familiar voice.

"Excuse me," said Alfie to one of the thugs. "Would you mind looking out the window at the parking lot? I believe you can see my Rolls-Bentley from here."

The man looked and nodded, his little pig eyes glittering.

"Take a look at the licence number," said Alfie. "Do the numbers happen to add up to seventeen?"

"No," said the thug. "Sixteen."

"Cor, stone the crows," said Alfie. "I was only a single digit away from winning the giant jackpot."

• • • • • •

"I suppose you're wondering why I've called you all here tonight!"

Garfield Cresswell, who had often been called a detective's detective (in his meteoric career he had captured twenty-seven detectives and brought them to justice) was speaking.

He turned and surveyed as motley a crew of weekenders as had ever come down for a weekend party here at Motley Manor on the downs: Major Sykes-Ffrith, DSO, tall and rumpled; Lady Pamela Snout, ravishing dowager; Gristle Makefast, well-known bookmaker; Sacheverell Famishing, noted novelist; young Reggie Faversham, apple of the Social Register; Grog Marvin, American TV star and rival (of Reggie) for the hand of lovely Listless Supine, exotic dancer; Riggs, the sneaky-looking butler; and last but not least, the much-despised and cordially hated Derek FitzCordial, who had been quite dead for thirty-six hours.

"One of you," said Garfield Cresswell, "is a murderer!" Outside the rain drummed ceaselessly on the leaden moonlight.

"The killer worked in a diabolical fashion," the detective continued. "This innocent-looking telephone was his weapon. When the telephone rang, somebody answered it, little realizing that—by this simple action—they were sealing Derek FitzCordial's doom. The lifting of the receiver set in motion an electrical impulse that triggered a mechanism that released a poisoned needle embedded in the victim's chair. You know the rest."

"But now," said Cresswell, "we shall use the same method to capture the killer *who at this moment is sitting in the self-same chair.* Only he and I know which it is. Five minutes from now I have arranged for that phone to ring, and then the killer must rise and reveal himself or suffer the fate of his victim."

Unexpectedly the phone rang, and the detective sprang at it with a curse. "Not yet, you fool!" he hissed into the receiver, but a familiar voice interrupted him with a cheery hello.

Garfield Cresswell slumped back in his chair with a muffled oath, his plan frustrated. Then he leaped into the air with a startled scream of pain. An instant later he was dead.

"Too bad," somebody murmured, picking up the receiver. "His phone number ended in a lucky 7. If he'd lived he would have won fifty silver dollars from good old CHOO."

The Adventures of
Harvey J. Fotheringham:
Space Detective

For all of the years in which I was a faithful reader of Buck Rogers, Flash Gordon and other futuristic comic heroes, one thing struck me forcibly: these young men had absolutely no home life. There was no Mom in the background, baking an electronic pie; there was no Wifey insisting on being taken along to the convention on Venus. There wasn't even a faithful dog, encased in the ubiquitous glass bubble, yapping at the heels of his master as he prepared for a death duel with the giant Tharks on Mongo.

There were girls, to be sure, but I noticed an odd thing about them: *they always wore the same outfit.* It was a sort of bathing suit with lapels. They did not seem to have a spring ensemble for their forays with the deadly Leopard Men of Mars. Nor was there anything resembling a fashionable fall frock. Most noticeable of all, they *never wore a hat!* I find it hard to believe that in the twenty-first century, women will not be wearing hats. And by that I do not mean that pilot's helmet thing with the visor that Wilma used to sport in the Buck Rogers strip. I mean something foolish, with feathers and lace.

When I start my own comic book all this will be corrected. I plan to begin it any day now if I can persuade Aislin of Montreal to handle the artwork. It will have an arresting title: *Harvey J. Fotheringham: Space Detective.* It will be a combination of Buck Rogers, Dick Tracy, and Dagwood.

Like all private eyes, past and futuristic, Harvey J. Fotheringham will operate from a cheap office on the 247th floor of the Interplanetary Building on Jupiter. And like all good private-eye stories, ours will begin when a beautiful blonde Mystery Woman walks into his office and calls him Bab-ee. Unfortunately for Harvey, this is the late twenty-first century: the Giant Two-Way Telescreen flashes on and a familiar voice calls out: *"Harv-eeeeee!"* It is Harvey's wife, dialing through from Earth.

As we all know from our constant study of science-fiction comic books and TV dramas, these two-way telescreens are a stock prop in the next millennium. Harvey has a miniature one shackled to his wrist and another in his private space-ship. Thus his wife is in constant touch with him, audio-visually speaking, warning him about pulling out too quickly on a red light, asking if he'd mind hopping over to Andromeda for a fresh bunch of grools for dinner, scolding him for taking the keys to the autogyro with him when he left for the office.

I think I will arrange to have an elevator strike in Harvey's building early in the game. I do not notice much about wage disputes in the present raft of science-fiction comics, and this will be a novelty for the kiddies. The operators will be striking for an extra million bucks a day (inflation having become something of a problem by then) and a fifteen-minute week.

This will give Harvey a chance to use his anti-gravity suit when leaving the office in pursuit of Black Rufe, Space Ghoul. As he leaps out of the window and strikes out for the parking lot he is almost decapitated by a two-seater rocket runabout. He ducks just in time to see the driver shake his fist and shout, "Fool pedestrians!"

Harvey's own machine is a three-year-old Chev Implausible (that's right, General Motors is still in business). It has seen better days and here, once again, my fresh approach to science-fiction comics will pay dividends. I notice in the present futuristic strips the spaceships are all brand new: they won't find a worn spot on the upholstery, either. Harvey's, however, will have a rather bad dent in its left tail fin and the paint job will be scratched. Actually, he would like to turn it in at Honest Dan's lot on the Moon, especially as a couple of the rockets are misfiring badly on cold mornings. But the Fotheringhams have been saving up for a summer place over Sirius way where the countryside is still unspoiled, so he'll have to make the old bus do for another year.

Harvey has got a hot tip that Black Rufe, Space Ghoul, may try to knock over the Fly-In Bank, which is a satellite full of money revolving around Uranus.

This bank (formerly known as the Toronto-Dominion-Royal-Montreal-Commerce-Nova Scotia-Barclay's-First National Bank of America) is not popular with Harvey, but it is the only bank left. He once tried to borrow a few measly millions to make a down payment on a disintegrator cannon, but the bank wouldn't look at him. Bring in collateral, the manager had said, and you can have funds at a mere 212 percent; Harvey had to go to the friendly Solar Finance Company. Still, duty is duty and he must hide his true feelings.

The traffic out to Uranus is sheer murder. It is Tuesday

and therefore a holiday for most people, along with Friday, Saturday, Sunday, Monday and Thursday. There are a lot of picnickers heading for the outer edge of the galaxy, where a new supply of fresh air has just been discovered.

Ever since the one-day week and thirty-minute day were introduced, all the radar lines from the Moon have been jammed. Harvey wonders, sometimes, if all this leisure time is good for people; wouldn't it be better to go back to the days when everyone worked a full hour a week? And this mad, radical talk of a fifteen-minute day? Sheer lunacy! The economy will never stand it, according to an editorial in the venerable *Financial Post*—a publication that clings to the Old Trusted Values.

Harvey has guessed Black Rufe's plan of strategy. The bandit will zoom in to the Fly-In Bank, approach the teller's cage and hand over a scrawled note reading: *"This is a stick-up! Dump loose bills into paper bag."* Stickups can be very costly in the twenty-first century since one shot from a disintegrator gun can demolish not only the Fly-In Bank but about half the planet, too. That's the trouble with atomic weapons: They've never been able to scale them down to size.

But Harvey means to frustrate the Space Ghoul. Sliding in beside Black Rufe, he is about to bring him to justice when a hand with a club in it appears from behind an old packing case. Fortunately, Mrs. Fotheringham, as always, is on the telescreen. *"Harv-eeeeee!"* she cries, and Harvey ducks just in time and pops Black Rufe in the snoot. I am going to have Aislin print the words **POW!** and **ZOWIE!** and then draw several stars over Black Rufe's head. And that's just about the end of the first episode except that the beautiful girl teller turns out to be the Mysterious Blonde we met earlier.

"Come here, Bab-ee," she says seductively.

Harvey is flitting over in his anti-gravity suit with a foolish smile on his face when a familiar voice is heard. *"Harv-eeeeee!"* shrills Mrs. Fotheringham. It's that damfool telescreen again.

Musical Interlude

TWO ODES FOR THE COLD WAR

An Ode to Sanitation

*Dedicated to the late U.S. President Dwight Eisenhower, who
at the time of Sputnik declared it was possible to produce a
"clean" nuclear bomb—i.e., one that would be relatively free
of fallout.*

As scientists, we must admit, the Russians have us beat
But there's one branch of research in which they can't
    compete;
Our plumbing is the envy of every Western nation:
We may not put up Sputniks—but we're tops at sanitation.
Oh, we invented Lifebuoy, when Stalin was a tot,
And we developed Listerine before the Czar was shot.
Now we've come up with MUM and BAN and DUZ and TIDE
    and VEL.
We only need one other thing to give those Russians hell:
So every last American, from Ike to Gravel Gertie,
Is praying that we'll soon perfect
A bomb that isn't dirty . . .

    We want a clean bomb—
    An absolutely antiseptic socially acceptable
        pristine bomb.
    Now war's a filthy business;
    We don't want it to recur,
    So we've got to have a clean bomb to
    Detergently deter.

We want a polite bomb!
Whiter than white bomb!
A bomb to knock the spots off that dirty Muscovite
　　bomb.
And if we have to drop it
You'll see our victims grin,
For we'll have the only H-bomb
That's made with Lanolin.

We want a clean bomb—
A tested-and-approved-by-*Good-Housekeeping*-
　　magazine bomb.
So when the mushroom cloud goes up
And folks die by the acre
They won't be plagued by Strontium-90
When they meet their Maker.

We want a demure bomb,
Safe and sure bomb,
A ninety-nine-and-forty-four-one-hundredths-percent
　　pure bomb.
And though our victims call out
Every time our bombs go past 'em,
We can promise that there won't be any
Fallout when we blast 'em.

As scientists, we must admit, the Russians have the edge,
But as leaders of the Western world, we make this
　　solemn pledge:

We'll keep sending chromium bathtubs to the Sikhs
    and Japanese;
We'll keep putting Cannon towels in every box of
    BREEZE;
We'll ship Kleenex to the Eskimos, although it may not
    suit 'em,
And if we're forced to bomb 'em, those bombs will not
    pollute 'em.

We want a clean bomb—
An undefiled, untarnished and untainted sweet-sixteen
    bomb.
Our enemies will thank us
For our faith in sanitation:
We may blow them all to pieces
But there'll be no radiation.

We want an okay bomb!
British fair play bomb!
With more active dirt remover than any other A-bomb.
Now Sani-Sealed in Pliofilm
To answer our demands,
When it finally explodes it won't
Be touched by human hands.

We want a clean bomb—
The kind-of-bomb-it's-safe-to-give-your-kids-on-
    Hallowe'en bomb.
Now that bomb may kill ten thousand

Little children in the night,
But when they lay those corpses out
They'll all be Rinso-white.

We want a chaste bomb!
An in-good-taste bomb!
An altogether ethical, high-principled, straitlaced
    bomb.
Our heritage is Puritan—
That's why we're dedicated;
Our high explosives, like our books
Are better expurgated.

As scientists, we must admit, the Russians are one-up,
But we invented Sani-Flush when Khrushchev was a pup.
They may have Sputniks in the air,
(We wince to hear them coming)
But we couldn't raise a satellite
Without the proper plumbing.
We can't stand contamination!
We consider it obscene!
And we'll never fight a dirty war
Without a bomb that's clean!

An Ode to Humanity:
Dedicated to the U.S. Air Force

"General Twining is *said to believe that the offshore islands provide the ideal conditions for demonstrating that small nuclear weapons can be used to fight and win a limited war. . . . Some of General Twining's advisers also say that this is a chance to prove that small nuclear weapons can be quite 'humane.'"* — Twentieth-century news item

Oh, in the world community
They say that opportunity
Knocks once, and then it never knocks no more;
So this chance to test munitions
Under limited conditions
We will never get again—unless there's war.

Though it sounds a bit extremish
There's no need to get all squeamish
For our weapons wouldn't really hurt a sheep;
Though we'll atomize those Reds
While they're snoring in their beds,
We guarantee it won't disturb their sleep.

Chorus:
And you really must admit
If you're noted for your wit
That when you're blown to pieces
It doesn't hurt a bit.

Now it's really for the best
That we make this small request:
Let us try a bomb or two upon that islet;
You may talk of a deterrent
But it ought to be apparent
It's more fun to drop an A-bomb than stockpile it.

> **Chorus:**
> *And though it's awesome to behold*
> *That mushroom cloud unfold,*
> *It won't really cause more torment*
> *Than a rather nasty cold.*

Now we've said it all before:
We're not advocating war;
If we did, we wouldn't blame 'em if they sacked us.
Though you call us each a dreamer
It's been years since Hiroshima
And it's time we had a little target practice.

> **Chorus:**
> *Oh, we'll sing it once again:*
> *We're terribly humane.*
> *We won't really cause more damage*
> *Than a bullet through the brain.*

Now it isn't much to ask
That we carry out our task—
After all, it's just a teeny-weenie bomblet;

Though its uncontrolled caprices
May blow tiny tots to pieces
Still you've got to break some eggs to make an omelet.

> **Chorus:**
> *And we can't be criticized,*
> *For, when all is analyzed,*
> *It doesn't really matter*
> *Just how you're pulverized.*

Now in simple Christian charity
We cannot stand barbarity
Base passion—we will always rise above it;
Our consciences are calm
We would never drop that bomb
If we weren't so very sure our victims love it.

> **Chorus:**
> *And there won't be any pain!*
> *For we're frightfully humane!*
> *If our enemies all die laughing*
> *Our work won't be in vain.*

Five

THE LITERARY LIFE

1. REVIEWING THE CLASSICS

*A Greek reviewer for the Sunday book page has these words
for a new best-seller, the* Odyssey *by Homer:*

Those who have waited with keen anticipation for Mr.
Homer's newest historical novel will, I fear, be sadly disap-
pointed by this sequel to the highly commended *Iliad.* In this
latest work Mr. Homer has done his best to duplicate his earlier success, but there is a sad lack of unity here that is scarcely masked by the orgy of blood-letting with which this author
seems to be obsessed. Let there be no mistake about one
thing: this sprawling novel—more travelogue than continuing story—will be a commercial success. Perhaps that will
satisfy its author. But one may venture to ask whether sheer
commercial favour is enough when applied to a man of Mr.
Homer's obvious gifts.

Mr. Homer has been determined, it would appear, to give
the public what it wants—a series of highly adventurous cos-
tume dramas, each patently episodic, and all starring his central figure, Odysseus. What bothers the serious reviewer here
is not so much the lurid melodrama as the fundamental lack
of deep characterization that one expects from the mature
writer. Cyclops, the one-eyed giant, is little more than a one-
dimensional caricature; Circe, for all her charm, is paper-
thin. Where is the real depth of feeling one would hope to

find in the three Sirens? Certainly one does not feel one really *knows* them well. Sadly one has to face facts: Homer has not lived up to his original promise.

• • • • • •

A critic for the local library journal reviews a new juvenile, Jack and the Beanstalk.

Anybody seriously interested in the development of young children's minds must surely deplore the trend to horror, violence, and cheap sensationalism evident in this latest offering. None of us really cares for "series" books at the best of times, since they tend to limit the child's own literary horizons. What is especially reprehensible here is that this latest in the "Jack" series maintains the brutality that put so many of us off in the earlier *Jack the Giant Killer*. Once again the story is dominated by a monster—and once again the monster meets a particularly bloody doom, this time by being smashed to pieces after a fall. The mind boggles at the effect of all this blood on young persons; worse, the cult of "violence for violence's sake" can easily warp the vision of immature readers. Theft, cupidity, murder—all are condoned in this juvenile; nor is there any shred of sentiment, any tatter of feeling, any depth of understanding for the giant himself. Not recommended.

• • • • • •

Athens' leading drama critic has some harsh words for Sophocles' latest potboiler, Oedipus Rex.

I have written before, and at some length, about the modern theatre's preoccupation with decadence. There is a cult among contemporary dramatists that seems concerned to the point of obsession with the "sick" elements in our midst. Everything that is seamy about the world today—all the sexual deviations, the refined forms of sadism, the dark neuroses, is grist for their mill. So let us bestow the accolade, if that is the word, on Mr. Sophocles: he has topped them all with his latest offering. Incest, black murder, self-inflicted torture of the most agonizing and bloody variety—all are here, laid out in the most explicit fashion for the unsqueamish playgoer.

All this might perhaps be forgiven the playwright were his tale believable. But *Oedipus Rex* does not ring true. Last night's credulous audience was asked to swallow the most patent coincidences, the most implausible dramatic situations.

The fact that Oedipus is married to a woman old enough to be his mother is not enough for Mr. Sophocles. Oh, no! She has to *be* his mother—and, mark you, we are asked to believe that the poor boob doesn't know it. And where, one finds oneself wondering, is papa all this time? We are finally told that Oedipus has murdered him—and he doesn't know *that*, either! It is pointless to continue. Suffice it to say that Mr. Sophocles' insatiable preoccupation with violence has led him into a ludicrously melodramatic ending. He has his hero, if you will believe it, gouge out his own eyes using the rings on his fingers! Need one say more?

● ● ● ● ● ●

A London theatre critic drops into the Globe to have a look at a new offering, Romeo and Juliet, *by one W. Shakespeare.*

The tendency to pander to the teenage crowd, and its resultant hazards, has never been better demonstrated than by this trifle. Indeed, one wonders why the management did not take the final step of titling the offering *I Married a Teenager*, since they obviously have a commercial success in mind. Mr. Shakespeare, a promising playwright in many ways, has chosen to make his lovers so young that they have scarcely achieved puberty; and there the play founders. His love poetry, from mature voices, might have had an eloquently romantic ring; but in the mouths of these children it is more than faintly ludicrous. As is usual in teen fables, both participants come to tragic ends—a climax that produces an audible amount of sniffling from the matinee crowd. No doubt we can expect the stickier of the romantic lyrics to make the Big Ten—which is exactly what the producers hope for. But I cannot recommend this pastiche for serious playgoers over the age of eighteen.

• • • • • •

And here, perhaps, is how the producers and publishers might have made use of the above reviews in their advertising:

THE ODYSSEY: ". . . an orgy of blood-letting . . . let there be no mistake about one thing: this . . . will be a commercial success . . . highly adventurous . . . deep characterization!"

JACK AND THE BEANSTALK: ". . . a story dominated by a monster! . . . the mind boggles!"

OEDIPUS REX: "Let us bestow the accolade . . . on Mr. Sophocles. He has topped them all! . . . Need one say more?"

ROMEO AND JULIET: ". . . obviously . . . a commercial success . . . eloquently romantic! . . . its lyrics (will) make the Big Ten! . . ."

2. FERENC STOKES, THE CRITICS' CRITIC

There was a testimonial dinner last week for Ferenc Stokes. Everybody was on hand to help honour the grand old man of the theatre on the occasion of his seventy-fifth birthday. It is a matter of considerable envy among his colleagues that no critic is hated and reviled so much as he.

Stokes has rightly been called the Critics' Critic. This is mainly because he does not stop at criticizing plays and movies and TV. He also criticizes critics.

Who can forget his telling commentary on one of the world's most celebrated drama reviewers?

I am at a loss to understand the cult which seems to hang on George Jean Nathan's every comma. Surely as a serious scrutineer of the antic arts (and by "serious" I mean something slightly more fibrous than the verbal buffoonery that passes for wit in our literary showrooms) he has long been found wanting. His shameless rhapsodizing over a minor O'Neill rewrite (*Mourning Becomes Electra*) stamps him as a man of mediocre perception while his stubborn espousal of playwrights of such limited ability as Sean O'Casey and Arthur Miller points to a lack of discrimination that would be shocking in a man of his supposed ideals and integrity were it not so palpable.

The secret of Stokes' success is astonishingly simple, as the above paragraph demonstrates. It wasn't that he was a good critic; he was simply a *different* critic. He always had the uncanny ability to figure out in advance what the other critics would say *and then he himself would say the exact opposite.* When Sir Laurence Olivier came to town you could depend upon Stokes to refer to him as "a much overrated actor." On the other hand, when reviewing TV he was quite likely to remark that "in spite of the prevailing opinion, *Buffy, The Vampire Slayer* is a workmanlike and appealing little program."

Stokes always defended his unorthodox opinions with such ferocity and aplomb that people (especially other critics) got the sneaking suspicion he might be right. Take for instance his original review of *My Fair Lady:*

> Outside of a fairly facile book, some rather derivative tunes and a couple of workmanlike performances by Stanley Holloway and Julie Andrews (that can on no account merit the adjective "great"), the divertissement at the Mark Hellinger is devoid of any real merit. No doubt the idea of raking over a popular, if overrated, potboiler by Shaw and turning it into a series of vaudeville turns, appeared meretricious on the surface; but Messrs Lerner and Loewe have yet to discover the truth that mere cleverness of theme is not enough. Let us agree that *My Fair Lady* (why that title, incidentally?) has the kind of mass appeal that drags the Broadway cultists from their lairs—they have come to expect the stereotype and the idea of an originally conceived and executed idea is anathema to them—but I simply cannot see this effusion passing into show business history.

After the success of *My Fair Lady*, Stokes might have been expected to recant. On the contrary, he attacked:

A return to *My Fair Lady* after some eighteen months bears out this corner's original contention (one, you may recall, that inspired some graceless derision at the time) that this effusion has no real staying power. Everybody is agreed by now, I think, that the show is the commercial success I predicted it would be; but to pretend anything more is to display a lack of critical acumen. It is a comment, I submit, on the general sterility of Broadway fare that this musical curiosity should continue to play to good houses in spite of the desultory nature of its theme and the general hackneyed quality of the music.

Whenever Stokes saw a performance that he knew would bring general critical condemnation, it was his practice to praise it. He was especially good at praising Grade B Monster Movies. His review of *Zombie in the Garret* is a case in point.

To those who profess to see great portent in the more vainglorious European films now cluttering up the art houses, I suppose *Zombie in the Garret* will be an object of sly ridicule. Yet, in its very simplicity and lack of pretension this quite candidly "commercial" film comes as a breath of fresh air after the thin obscurities of Bergman and the souped-up symbolism of Fellini. Say what you will about Nanook J. Screel, minor director though he may be, at least he brings to this small gem of a picture a sure professionalism of touch that is sadly lacking in our so-called "message" films. *Zombie in the Garret* may not be Great Art (whatever that is), but at least it is sound entertainment. Its progenitors know exactly what they are doing and, within their own limits, they do it well. And after all, what is so wrong with sound entertainment?

Stokes, I've often thought, was at his best when handling amateur groups. Generally he tore them to pieces with a savagery usually reserved for the Katherine Cornells and the Tennessee Williamses of this world. But it was his habit, once each year, to "discover" some wretched hole-in-the-wall group of mummers and praise them to the skies. This so unnerved other critics that for days after they would traipse about town looking for the attic or the basement that Stokes had somehow managed to turn into a shrine:

Do not hesitate *[Stokes once wrote]* to make your pilgrimage to that hayloft in Ajax where a scandalously underpublicized group of inspired young people have succeeded in performing the kind of theatrical miracle that their professional colleagues have sadly failed to bring off. Never mind that the acting is primitive, the sets non-existent, the seating clumsy, and the acoustics less than satisfactory. Never mind that the play lacks any semblance of plot and depends entirely on the whim of the directors and the nightly improvisations

of the actors. Never mind that the performers themselves are all under the age of eighteen. All this is quite
irrelevant. What matters is that there is a spontaneity
here, a freshness of approach, a verve such as we have
not witnessed in the environs since I called the public's attention to the Ashcan Players' vastly underrat-
ed production of *East Lynne*. I think we may expect
great things of the young director Fortescue Wheem,
if he does not succumb to those false gods that have
lured so many of his predecessors from the path . . .

As a result of this one review, Fortescue Wheem became
the most sought-after director in town and moved on to New
York, where he became involved in a play that won a critics'
year-end award. Stokes of course was present to watch his
discovery in action:

As predicted here some time ago, Fortescue Wheem
has not lived up to that earlier promise that one or two
of us thought he showed. His present work displays
all the tawdriness and lack of inspiration that we have
come to associate with a Tyrone Guthrie or an Elia
Kazan. Granted that he has assembled a sackful of
cheap theatrical tricks, but he has yet to learn the truth
that in the theatre mere gimmickry is not enough . . .

It was, as Wheem later said, the supreme accolade.

Exclusive! First-person
Revelations from the
Popular Press

I WAS QUEEN ELIZABETH'S
CHAMBERMAID'S FORMER BOYFRIEND
by Dwight G. Fenwicke

I have decided at last, in spite of Palace strictures and an oath of secrecy, to reveal all. I do this not only because I believe the people within the Palace are human beings with human emotions, human foibles and human cares, and that they need to be humanized, but also because I am human, too, and need the dough.

I remember the first time I met Bessie Perkins, the Queen's third chambermaid. It was in the Dog & Drone, a public house in Pimlico in the very shadow of that glamorous edifice that we "insiders" like to refer to affectionately as "Buck House."

And it was there, that very day, that Bessie Perkins revealed to me and to me alone one of the little-known secrets of the Palace, an intimate sidelight on Palace life that I intend to disclose in these memoirs exclusively and for the first time.

Bessie was seated demurely in a corner of the pub when I entered, toying with a gin and orange. I like to enter pubs toying with a gin and orange. I do it for effect.

"Hello, old girl," says I to her, for she was seventy-two if she was a day.

"Garn!" says she, in her quaint fashion—and that expression told me a world about her. It told me that she had been to the matinee performance of *My Fair Lady*.

We struck up a conversation and it was then that I learned the first of many secrets about the Royal Family that I plan to reveal frankly, openly and for money in these memoirs.

The Queen, Bessie whispered, sleeps between *white sheets!* With every colour of the rainbow to choose from these days, Her Majesty prefers the pristine, chaste, conservative colour of fine, bleached linen. What could be more fitting for a royal monarch? What could be more royal?

In a world gone mad with colour, it is significant, I think, that Her Majesty has chosen to return to Essential Things. It tells us something about her inner character and personality—not much, but something.

(In tomorrow's gripping instalment, Dwight G. Fenwicke, from his listening post at the Dog & Drone, will reveal another exclusive, little-known fact about the royal domicile that throws a fascinating new light on the complicated yet essentially simple character of Queen Elizabeth II.)

I WAS PRINCE PHILIP'S FORMER VALET'S FORMER BARBER
by Osmunde G. Sykes

I shall never forget the morning, at about a quarter before twelve, when young Piltdown, the Duke's valet, first entered my barbershop. I was just putting the finishing touches on a really British haircut for an American executive—chopping the locks off in the "waterfall" style, which no amount of later barbering can ever quite eliminate. The Yank's curses were still echoing from the walls when the youth stepped into the chair and asked for a manicure.

I liked his looks from the first moment. I think it bespeaks Prince Philip's essentially human side that he should have selected this obviously sensitive young person as his valet.

Not only was young Piltdown faultlessly attired but there was also a literary turn to his speech that I found attractive. He talked knowingly of Joyce and Proust and slowly, as I won his confidence, I was able to worm out of him the intelligence that he himself was engaged in a literary work.

It says something for Prince Philip, I think, that he should have employed a valet who could write. How many princes have we known who stubbornly insisted on hiring valets who were entirely illiterate and could not so much as sign their own name!

And now, in this exclusive memoir, I wish to reveal a hitherto unpublished fact about Prince Philip and his valet, a fact that casts new light on the complicated and yet intensely human relations that exist within the walls of the Palace.

Prince Philip's valet's first book is to be titled, "I Was Prince Philip's Valet." Notice here the correctness of the grammar, the scrupulous use of the verb in the past tense rather than the present. It is correct because Prince Philip has just fired his valet and got himself a new man who has to sign his name with an X. I think this tells us something about Prince Philip's character. I'm not certain, but I think so.

(In tomorrow's exciting instalment, Osmunde G. Sykes will reveal another exclusive, little-known fact about Prince Philip's former valet.)

I WAS PETER TOWNSEND'S FORMER ASSISTANT AUTO MECHANIC
by Derek G. Fanshawe

I should like to begin this exclusive series by stating frankly that I have no interest at all in cheap, salacious gossip of the kind usually connected with memoirs of this nature. I should like to begin that way, but, unfortunately, I can't.

But let me say at the outset that Peter Townsend was greatly misunderstood. This was especially true when we passed through Northern M'jomboland and he tried to speak to the natives in their native Svengali. I doubt if one out of ten understood him. He was also greatly misunderstood in Fiji, Somaliland, and Brooklyn.

I am often asked if he spoke of Princess Margaret during our drive through the fern forests that border the crater of Hawaii's Kilauea. I am often asked if he gazed at her photograph during our tour by jeep across the African veldt. And did he whisper her name when we stood on the edge of the mountain vastness that is Kilimanjaro? To these questions I can give a simple and, I hope, frank answer: No.

But I do recall a moving conversation I had with him in the headhunting regions of Upper New Guinea. It would be a betrayal of confidence if I were to repeat this conversation here, so I shall repeat it.

"Let's get moving," Townsend said to me, and the bleak way in which he said it and the tautness of his face spoke volumes. That is the kind of man Peter Townsend is—or was before he fired me. That is the secret of his essential humanity.

(In tomorrow's exclusive instalment, Derek G. Fanshawe tells another moving story about the lonely, misunderstood but essentially human man known as Peter Townsend.)

Meaningless Laudations
for Book Jackets

It was our century that saw the invention of the Book Jacket Club, in which every newly published novel contained on its dust cover several enthusiastic reviews composed not by real book critics but by friends of the author. The problem haunts everybody in the business. What do you do if a pal asks you to write a plug for the flap copy of his newest work and you find that you hate it? How do you keep your friend and yet satisfy your own conscience? The only solution is to write a critique that, while highly laudatory, will also be unusable. This requires all the skill of a tightrope walker, but it's possible to bring it off, as the following blurbs from recent works demonstrate.

•••••••

Though undeniably the work of an immature craftsman. Sacheverell Pike's massive novel *In Dubious Taste* shows that we have a developing writer in our midst. The flaws here—if we may call them that—are flaws in the right direction: they are the flaws of the beginner, and we may expect to see them corrected with time. What the book lacks in professional quality it more than makes up for in its youthful exuberance. We may expect great things from Mr. Pike in the future and the fact that he is seventy-two should in no way diminish our pleasure in discovering a new and hitherto hidden talent.

•••••••

The thing that struck me very forcibly about Ronald Sheffield's remarkable novel, *Make Haste to Stay,* is the high quality of craftsmanship displayed by the publisher. The jacket is a work of pure joy while the binding is a particularly fine example of the book manufacturer's art, being pleasing to the eye while at the same time grease-resistant. The type is large and clear, the margins wide without being obstreperous, and the title pages neatly and logically arranged to give maximum display. The book itself is remarkably free of those typographical errors that madden the lay reader and professional alike. All in all a worthwhile volume.

• • • • • •

The chief quality of Farley Hench's novel, *That Rackstraw Woman!* it seems to me, is that it is the sort of book you can give your teenage daughter to read without the slightest fear that it will corrupt her. This little volume is remarkably free of those scenes of passion and intimate relationship that have sullied the names of Lawrence and Miller. Although it deals with the interplay between men and women, I do not believe that that overworked word "sex" ever appears between the covers, nor is there the slightest hint in the narrative itself of any untoward incidents between the major characters. The men behave as gentlemen should while the women are perfect ladies in the best sense of the word. This is a book that can be read aloud at Home and School meetings and Boy Scout Father and Son nights alike without bringing a blush to the most sensitive cheek. A healthy, clean, wholesome story, in short, simply told in Mr. Hench's admirably unadorned and straightforward style.

• • • • • •

It is a joy to those of a scholastic turn of mind to come upon an author whose respect for that oft-discarded literary device, the footnote, has not been diluted by a craving for cheap popularity. It is true that Rodney Atwood's use of footnotes in his exhaustive *Fiasco at Harper's Ferry* tends to slow the narrative line and occasionally bring it to a dead stop, but this is a small price to pay for the erudition displayed. One must needs credit Mr. Atwood with something of a tour de force on page 1016, which contains no fewer than twenty-seven footnotes, including four Op. cit.s and thirteen Ibids., leaving room for only one line of narrative proper. Again, few living writers can match the footnote that begins on page 986 and runs for seventeen pages before coming to a halt. I know of no other volume about the Civil War so carefully annotated as Mr. Atwood's, and readers who are able to pick it up can do so with the assurance that they are getting the full story. This volume is an absolute must as a door stop.

• • • • • •

In these days of sweeping historical novels writ large in a sort of verbal Cinemascope, it comes as a relief to pick up a little tale told on a small canvas. Anthony Stoddard's *Wellington at Waterloo* has the quality of an exquisite miniature. The author has wisely avoided the pitfalls of earlier biographers who, in attempting to capture the sweep and drama of the great battle, have missed the essential qualities of the man himself. Those readers who are looking for an adventure story filled with heroic deeds on the battlefield or a tale of political intrigue, sibilant with the whispers of Whitehall, will not find it here. Mr. Stoddard, who has sensibly limited his research to a careful reading of the *Encyclopedia Britannica*, does not clutter his book with clever anecdotes or witty stories. Instead he concentrates on tiny facets of Wellington's family life, such as their theories (now happily obsolete) on the rearing of babies. The trick of omitting the entire battle itself and substituting instead the symbolism of sunrise over the Thames is a device that future historians will do well to examine carefully before discarding. By confining all the action to the interior of the saloon bar of a London pub, Mr. Stoddard has made his little book easily adaptable to a one-act play suitable for performance by high school dramatic groups and others.

•••••

In Ethelred Krafft-Schemling, we are witnessing the debut of a new mystery writer and one who is certain to leave his mark on the world's detective fiction. Critics may cavil at his uncompromising insistence on revealing the identity of the murderer as early as Chapter Three in *Corpse on Seventh Avenue*, but there is little doubt that this radical approach will stimulate new controversy and interest in a form of storytelling that was beginning to show signs of advancing age. (For the reader, of course, it pays big dividends since he does not need to finish the remainder of the book.) One cannot help but admire the author's no-nonsense approach to the puzzle of the murder. On the opening page the reader is led into believing that the butler did it: what a tantalizing surprise, then, to discover, in the denouement, that the butler really *did* do it! But rather than spoil the plot, I will not go into details. Suffice it to say that this is a book.

Letters Ann Landers Wouldn't Print

Do you remember Ann Landers? Of course you do. She's alive and still dispensing advice to the wretched of the earth, who hang on her every word even though she's now slightly in the shadow of someone who calls herself Miss Manners. The most tantalizing aspect of the Landers canon, however, is the letters that she answers but *does not print.* Every once in a while, if you're a faithful reader, you'll notice there's a "confidential" reply to some unnamed seeker after advice. Although these are always intriguing, it's maddening to wonder what the *question* was. It is possible, however, to piece together some of these letters by reading between the lines of the answers. Here are some actual examples, with Miss Landers' printed remarks in italics.

CONFIDENTIAL to Sorry for Her: If you give her what she wants only because she has the tear ducts of an orphaned onion-peeler, then you're the dunce.

THE LETTER: Dear Ann Landers—I have been taking out this certain party for seventeen years and have thought recently in terms of matrimony. However, one small thing bothers me. She cries a lot. When we first started dating I noticed that tears often streamed down her face when we met. I put this down to some defect in my own appearance, but since she accepted my attentions in a not unwelcome manner I was forced to the conclusion that her early upbringing in an orphanage was preying on her mind. As the years rolled by, I slowly reconciled myself to streaky mascara and salty kisses. Recently, however, I have stumbled upon the horrible truth: my bride-to-be is employed as a peeler in a mammoth Instant Onion factory. This explains the constant tears and also an odour redolent of the midway that escaped my notice in the first flushes of ardour. With this knowledge, should I yield to her desires or am I being a dunce? After all, an onion-peeler is beneath me socially. Signed: **Sorry for Her.**

• • • • • •

CONFIDENTIAL to Want to Help: This girl needs more help than you give her during coffee breaks. It sounds as if her mother gave her an inferiority complex for a birthday present. She should have therapy.

THE LETTER: Dear Ann Landers—I am an award-winning producer of Class B monster pictures here in Hollywood and I have a problem. There is this very attractive bit player who I have been trying to help by giving fatherly advice during coffee breaks on the set. I have told her if she will only play ball with me I can get her the lead in *The Creature from the Utter Depths*. Honestly, she is perfect for the role with a little evening coaching from yours truly. However, she doesn't see it, and I believe she has come under the evil influence of a possessive mother who has convinced her to shun me. I want to help but need guidance as to how to proceed. Signed: **Want to Help.**

• • • • • •

R.W.G.: Perfection itself can be a flaw. Do your best. Angels can do no more.

THE LETTER: Dear Ann Landers—For some time now

I have felt that I am being socially ostracized by others in my peer group, so I turn to you for advice and comfort. Ever since my betrothal to Carmelino Oobleck of the world-famous Ooblecks, my affianced has been trying to teach me the rudiments of high-wire trapeze work. There are five Ooblecks at present, and they wish to include me in the act after our marriage. They form this human pyramid while balancing on a set of bottles that are teetering on a slack wire fifty feet above the centre ring. The idea is for me to stand on the top of this human pyramid and juggle eight basketballs. It is a very good act, but I am afraid that I'm all thumbs. I just can't get the hang of it and as a result have suffered two broken collarbones, a fractured kneecap, a bruised spleen, several contusions and the opprobrium of my colleagues. Poor Carmelino is getting impatient with me for not attaining perfection and is already making eyes at the girl on the flying trapeze, "Angels" Rathgeb. What do you say? Signed: **R.W.G.**

• • • • • •

CONFIDENTIAL to Can't Control It: You have "black cord fever." I strongly recommend that you have your telephone disconnected until you get over this compulsion.

THE LETTER: Dear Ann Landers—I am turning to you for help in a matter of the heart since my psychiatrist simply doesn't understand me. He says I have a rare case of "black cord fever," a hallucinatory disease that he claims I contracted on a recent visit to the Bight of Biafra. I say he is dead wrong. He tells me that I only think I'm a telephone, but I *know* I'm a telephone. I say this because there is another telephone living at our house and I have fallen in love with her. She's a real Princess. I think she is trying to tell me something because she rings constantly, but so far I haven't been able to communicate. What is the correct etiquette in such cases? Signed: **Can't Control It.**

• • • • • •

CONFIDENTIAL to Ashamed of Them: Well, how do you suppose your "ignorant, ill-bred, pig-like parents" raised such a refined, elegant young gentleman as you? Think it over.

THE LETTER: Dear Ann Landers—I am the product of a very strange upbringing. Taken to India at seven months by my parents, Lt.-Col. and Mrs. The Hon. Bartleigh Ffoulkes-Welphnashier, I might have been raised in the luxury generally accorded to the scion of a noble line had it not been for one of those weird mishaps that pepper the works of romantic fiction. My real parents were swept overboard when our ship foundered with all hands. Flung on a sandy jungle shore, more dead than alive, I found myself ensconced in a colony of wild pigs, which are common to these parts. Two of them became my foster parents, and as far as I was concerned they were "Mom" and "Dad." Brought up as one of their own, I spoke only in grunts until I reached the age of eighteen when I met in the jungle the beautiful young daughter of a white hunter whom I learned to love. It was she who taught me the rudiments of language, beginning with simple phrases such as "Me, Jane; you, You" and working up, as timed passed, to lengthy discussions on the love theories of Reik. I in turn taught her the art of wallowing. Time came, however, when I must needs return to London to claim my rightful heritage as Lord Greysmear. Here, in a gentlemen's club, I learned refinements and elegance. Now this brings me to my problem. "Mom" and "Dad" have expressed a desire to leave the jungle and visit me at my digs. Will they be accepted for what they are here at the Mother of Nations? Or will some of my friends consider them (as I do) ignorant, ill-bred, and let's face it, uncommonly pig-like? Signed: **Ashamed of Them.**

Best-Sellers We
Never Got to Read

These typical twentieth-century hard covers are still available on the remainder tables of some of the shabbier second-hand dealers.

Too Old To Die, Too Young To Weep

A decade ago Francenella Kincaid was the brightest young star on the Broadway-Hollywood orbit. Tabbed for greatness as a torch singer, dramatic actress, tap dancer, and mime, the darling of café society and a *Cosmo* cover girl, she suddenly faded into obscurity. Why? Here, in a sympathetically and honestly told confession (to Gerald Frank), she reveals every stark detail of the weird, often shocking story about a strange addiction, which has heretofore only been discussed in whispers. Timed nicely to coincide with Miss Kincaid's comeback, the book is a literary experience no housewife will want to miss.

I Was Ernest Hemingway's Gardener

This is a revealing book about one of our literary giants by the only man who could tell it. Jimsey Rathscail worked seven summers on the Hemingway estate planting petunias and coreopsis, and in this intimate work he reveals a little-known facet of the Hemingway personality—the fact that Hemingway himself had absolutely no interest in gardening and indeed did not speak more than three words to his gardener during all that time. This is not just another book of Hemingway revelations; it is the same book.

The Biggest Story Ever Told

The publishers have already announced in prepublication statements that this sprawling novel of love, lust, sex, abortion, incest, and religion is the "Big Book" of the year. They base their claim on the fact that the novel runs 2,013 pages and is so heavy that a free Loblaws cart is being given away with each copy. One hundred thousand have already been contracted for, and two book clubs have merged in order to be able to handle the volume. Based loosely on Biblical events, it is the combined work of Danielle Steel and Scott Turow, who wrote alternate chapters. A must as a flower presser.

Fatness Is Good for You!

Certain to be one of the most discussed of the twenty-seven books on diet being published this season, this controversial treatise by a discredited doctor will be welcomed by all who are baffled and enraged by the current slimming craze. Rheinhold Schneir, M.D., now unveils a new diet that allows you to *eat all you want.* Indeed, the first 450 pages simply consist of a list of OK foods. It is Schneir's thesis that even if his diet cuts fifteen years off your life, you'll die happy and contented. Banned by the American Medical Association, it is certain to rise swiftly to the top of the best-seller list.

A Subtreasury of Joyce, Miller and Lawrence

Here's a handy little volume that every book-lover will cherish. Timed for the Christmas trade, it contains a careful culling of *all* "controversial" passages from the once-banned works of the three most discussed authors of our time. Readers who want to examine certain sections of these world-renowned classics will be able to get them in this one volume, thus saving the price of a small library of erotica. In a lengthy preface the editors go to some lengths to explain that their purpose is entirely scholarly and that they have no intention of indulging in sensation for sensation's sake. To make this position unequivocally clear they have stamped on the cover in large red letters the words "NOT SOLD TO ANYONE UNDER THE AGE OF 12."

Ernest Hemingway Was My Gardener

Even learned Hemingway scholars will be surprised to read that their literary hero once toiled briefly as a gardener on a sumptuous Long Island estate. Now in this revealing volume, which casts new light on the early life of our most famous novelist, Ferrold Ramshackle tells with wit and insight something of his experiences with young Hemingway. In doing so he reveals that Hemingway had absolutely no interest in gardening and, indeed, hardly exchanged a word with his employer in the days before he was fired. A must for Hemingway buffs.

The Marilyn Monroe Suicide Hoax

This is slated to be one of the most sensational "exposé" books of the season and certainly timed for "up-to-the-minute" news copy. Ace Hollywood reporter Gary Slurb has spent literally hours digging into the background of the tragic Monroe case, and he now advances the startling theory—

founded to a large degree on actual evidence—that Miss Monroe did not die of an overdose of sleeping pills but is actually alive and in hiding somewhere in South America. Hollywood has already bought the book as a starring vehicle for Francenella Kincaid.

When the Queen Went Naked

A superb treatise on butterfly hunting in the Melanesian Group, this slim volume is certain to attract attention because of its evocative title. The "Queen," of course, is a rare butterfly. An especially attractive dust jacket shows naked Melanesian lepidopterists gambolling in the surf. Great for window displays during a lull.

How to Make Your First $100,000

In this remarkable "do-it-yourself" volume, Ancaster Grasp explains in detail how he made $100,000 in royalties from his last book, *How to Make a Million Dollars in Your Spare Time*. He tells his readers how they can write similar books with equally remunerative results. Certain to be a best-seller.

Magazine Titles That Sell

Those who dance on the periphery of the magazine world know that the secret of a successful magazine is to come up with titles so compelling that every customer will be forced to read at least a paragraph of the story that follows. The spin doctors who advise magazine editors make it clear that their readers are interested in five basic subjects: themselves, children, dogs, sex, and crime. It is, of course, standard practice in the business to think of a title first and then hire some aspiring freelancer to give it shape. Here, then, free of charge, are some suggestions that the Periodical Writers Association of Canada may wish to publish in an upcoming issue of their chapbook.

Title: IS YOUR CHILD'S DOG A SEX CRIMINAL?

Subtitle: Here's a frank, hard-hitting report that no parent can afford to miss. A world-famous psychiatrist pulls no punches as he examines both sides of the most controversial problem of our times. His findings may surprise you.

Exclusive!

Title: ADOLF EICHMANN WAS MY MOTHER

Subtitle: Here, for the first time, is a little-known sidelight on the bizarre life of the most hated Nazi of our time. Though these revelations may shock you, we publish them here as a revealing human document and a warning to the future.

Title: I MARRIED A ZOMBIE
        Another true personal experience
Subtitle: From the steaming jungles of Haiti comes the heart-warming, intensely human story of a strange marriage they said would never work. No young bride will want to miss the inspirational tale of how one young couple achieved the impossible through prayer.

Title: DOES CANCER CAUSE SMOKING?
Subtitle: Here's new hope for nicotine addicts. Impressive new scientific tests now suggest that your craving for tobacco may merely be the result of incipient cancer. An exclusive behind-the-scenes report on a major scientific breakthrough.

Title: WE DROVE TO TIERRA DEL FUEGO
        BY CANOE
Subtitle: Here's the rollicking tale of an unusual family who decided to enjoy a holiday that was "different." You'll love this high-spirited and intensely human story of a memorable vacation—told by the sole survivor.

Title: SHOULD TEENAGERS COMMIT ADULTERY?
Subtitle: "Yes!" says one member of our community panel. "No!" thunders another. Between these two extreme points of view the pros and cons of a hitherto hush-hush subject are weighed and brought frankly into the open.

Title: TRANS-CANADA ROMANCE
        An All-Canadian Award-Winning Story

Subtitle: When Halifax-born Reggie met lovely Marcia from Moose Jaw on a beach in Vancouver, he did not know she was leaving that night for Saskatoon. But then he succumbed to the charms of a wistful Québécoise from Trois-Pistoles . . .

Title: AT LAST! AN ECONOMY DIET THAT
        REALLY TAKES OFF POUNDS

Subtitle: Exhaustive wartime tests at Belsen and Auschwitz now prove beyond doubt that the controversial "sawdust diet" really works—and is easy on your food budget, too. Here's a revolutionary method of losing weight that actually saves you money.

So if any up-and-coming editor is short of ideas he can have these absolutely free. My own magazine days are over.

A New Work of
Imaginative Fiction

A special Governor General's Award for creative fiction will almost certainly be made sometime this month, Canadian Press revealed today.

The award is to be given to a Mr. P. Berton for his most recent expense account, which has been hailed as "the most sensitive and imaginative work of fiction yet to come from the pen of a Canadian author."

Mr. Berton, ever modest, said the expense account would not have been possible had he not been able to build on the genius of others who had gone before.

Although the prizewinning work was completed in a white heat after a mere sixty-five hours of intensive creative application, it was really the product of a "lifetime of thought and contemplation."

He had, he said, torn up the present MS on three occasions and begun anew because the earlier drafts were, as he described it, "unrewarding."

He said that the final draft was "fairly satisfactory," but added that no creative writer is ever fully satisfied with what he has produced.

"Even after the thing was completed and signed I felt I wanted to fiddle with it—adding a dollar here, a fifty-cent piece there," he told the press. "Needless to say, I resisted the temptation. An expense account scratched over is an expense account lacking in authority."

Mr. Berton said he had been fiddling with expense

accounts for years and enjoying little success.

"They kept being sent back, time and time again, for revision," he recalls, going back to those hard days of struggle as a tyro expense-account writer.

"Then one day an expense account of mine accidentally got mixed up with a pile of manuscripts being judged for the *Maclean's* fiction contest. The judges unanimously awarded it a second prize, commenting on its 'sheer daring and stark drama.' Unfortunately, as I was at the time on the staff of the magazine and the expense account had actually been entered for a brief trip to Hamilton, the prize had to be withdrawn. So did the expense account. Yet it gave me the courage to go on—to create."

Critics have been unanimous in their praise of the present expense account and have hailed Berton's impressive development over the years.

"This newer, longer work justifies the promise shown by the younger Berton in briefer journeys to Oshawa, Belleville, and Woodbridge," says the West Elbow *Star-Graphic-Times*, in a glowing review. "Here we have the mature Berton—sophisticated, generous and, above all, imaginative—travelling to the far corners of the world and begrudging nothing. The **Miscellaneous** section alone justifies the prophecy that we are witnessing, on the Canadian scene, the full flowering of a major talent."

"The **Miscellaneous** section is sheer poetry!" says the Webfoot *Graphic-Times-Star*. "The single curt entry, **Saddle Soap: 52 cents**, speaks volumes."

"If Berton had done nothing more than compose that

lyrical and haunting passage listed as **Sundries**, I venture to suggest we should still feel warranted in bestowing upon him the accolade for the most elastic and furtive mind of our times," bubbles William Arthur Grebe in the Grillwater *Courier-Intelligencer-Expositor and Co-ordinator.*

Many critics commented approvingly on the fact that Berton had kept every item listed under **Sundries** to less than five dollars.

"A swift glance at the section suggests that this is a man careful with the firm's money to the point of fanaticism," writes F.J. Groyne-Phillips in the Canadian *Chartered Accountant.* "Only the most practised eye would realize that there are actually 567 items listed under **Sundries**."

Another bold and imaginative innovation, hailed by the *Canadian Actuarial Review* as a "giant step backward," is Berton's "spirited rejection of round numbers in this voluminous but meticulous work. Over and over again one sees such intriguing figures as '$2.34 . . . $4.61' and even '$3.99.' Says the *Review*, with grudging admiration: "The author here has borrowed the pricing techniques of other media to lend a gloss of authenticity to an otherwise preposterous work."

"Berton's handling of the **Incidentals** section, usually a disaster in fiction of this kind, shows the sure, firm sense of purpose that bespeaks a mature and experienced talent," says the Grogstart *Gazette and Post-Connubial.* "One can recall the days when his touch was not so sure, his technique almost faltering. It takes a man of bold imagination to write: '**Hiring a helicopter to inspect Epsom Derby: $23.29.**' Berton seems to have pulled it off."

"What volumes this work speaks!" enthuses the Grebesville *Streak*. "The reader is treated to a glittering array of restaurants, conducted through the lobbies of some of the world's most expensive hotels; introduced, at lunch and dinner, to a fascinating array of characters, all of them gourmets of the highest order."

It is Berton's sure sense of characterization that comes to the fore in his deceptively skilful handling of the **Entertainment** section, a piece of creative writing that thrilled many reviewers.

"Gone are the 'J. Smiths' and 'R. Joneses' of the earlier works," says the Frenstart *Times-Orifice*. "Gone are the simple notations for lunch or ent. Berton's technique is impressively seen in such entries as '**Post-breakfast port and cigars with Sir Reginald Wells-Greisleight re: Page 367 London Morality Report . . . $2.36,**' or again, '**Pre-luncheon sherry and canapés with Miss Erotica LaVerne re: Investigation London Club situation (Soho), first phase only . . . $4.21.**'

A brief passage, plucked at random from the much discussed **Incidentals** section, serves to show, as nothing else can, Berton's amazing range in subject matter and technique:

Calming head waiter **$3.12**
Replacing collar stud . . . . **$2.03 (tax incl.)**
Nerve pills . . . . **$4.59 (no tax)**
Tomato juice . . . . **$ .11**
Rent of elevator **$4.13**
Rope @ 34 cents ft.; 10 ft. **$3.40**

Comments, meanwhile, are still pouring in.

". . . exciting . . . "

        — Philip Marchand, *Toronto Star.*

". . . inventive . . . "

        — Yvonne Crittenden, *Toronto Sun.*

". . . quite . . . "

        — Robert Fulford, *Globe.*

". . . outrageous . . . "

        — J.R. Grebe, Chief Accountant, Price Waterhouse.

The Novel of
the Century

There was a time in Canada when everybody seemed to be writing a novel. Or, to put it more accurately, "working on a novel"—a phrase that covers a multitude of omissions. At one point in my career I was actually working on about fifteen novels and had, indeed, written the beginnings for them all. I was especially good at opening paragraphs. The trouble was I could never get any farther.

Here for instance, are the opening paragraphs for a daring novel of young love in the sunshine, so sexy and so expensive that even the Toronto Public Library, with all its resources, will not be able to afford it:

> The house where Matthew lived out his ninety-seven years was one of those mouldering Rosedale mansions, turreted and bay-windowed, that had seen robust days and was now entering its second childhood, sticky with the fingerprints of children long grown old and rank with the smell of new death.
>
> The world whistled by the Old Snarf Place, as the old-timers called it; it was so much a part of Rosedale that few paid it heed, or bestowed upon it the ultimate favour of a second glance. Its windows, shuttered and lace-curtained against the intruding sun, gazed sightless upon the children gamboling among the hedges of pigweed, which had long since blurred the edges of ancient brick.

Occasionally, there were murmurs of mysterious (some said sinister) rites held within the dark cavern, behind the crumbling façade; but few paid them heed. Every house has its ghosts; the Old Snarf Place was no exception. It was only when Jed Rudebago returned—"young Mr. Jed," as he was once known—that the outside world learned the truth . . .

That, I fear, is as far as I ever got with my epic novel, "Don't Cry Those Tears Away." What about young Mr. Jed? What did he discover? What *was* the secret of the Old Snarf Place? And when do we get to the part about young love in the springtime? I wish I could answer those questions, but I am as much in the dark as you.

Here are the opening lines of another novel, a slim tome entitled "Brief Candle," which, if it is ever completed, will undoubtedly be sold to the movies, rewritten entirely and issued under the title of "Love and Mamie Forsythe."

She lay, plangent and alone, in the enormous bed, her breath issuing weakly from her pale lips like a drying breeze on a July day. The night nurse had stepped out for a moment and she was alone in the room—alone in this room that, in every sense, had been her life.

Somewhere in the distance a gramophone scratched a pale comment about love and the stars above. Three storeys below, a dog uttered a guttural punctuation mark. And then, as her ears became attuned to the unaccustomed quiet, she heard for the first time the cadence of low conversation in the adjoining room.

She strained to catch its gist and, straining, lost her breath and lay gasping among the cool sheets. For a moment she thought the end had come, but, by an effort of will, she raised herself and listened once more. There was no mistaking it: they were talking about her. She uttered a muffled curse and swore a terrible oath. *I will not die this night,* she said, *no, nor for many nights to come. I will not give them the satisfaction . . .*

Sort of tugs at your heart strings, doesn't it? It sure tugged at mine. If I had two hundred and fifty pages like it, I could retire to a small island off Spain where the other novelists are. I wish I knew what happened next. Apart from everything else, I'm sort of curious. But I don't really know.

Here's one I particularly like:

The corpse lay face down, and you could see by the knife in its back and the condition of the head that it was deader than a mackerel. Mike O'Snarf knelt beside it, cold anger rising within him. In the distance he could still hear the pounding of the surf. The police would be here in minutes, but first, he had to know. He picked the body up by the midriff and turned it over. With a gasp he reeled back. This was no cheap gangster, shot in a mob war; this was a woman! She was very blonde and very pale and very, very beautiful. And Mike O'Snarf, private investigator, staring into the dead face, realized with a pang that he loved her . . .

I started a novel the other day that I rather like. It has an exotic foreign background:

Tim Carstairs stopped for a moment on the heights overlooking the *walabi*, reached into the folds of his chalk white *warabia*, produced his pipe and, gazing at the jungle below, indulged in a quiet smoke. His clean, firm profile cut the hard blue of the tropical sky as sharply as a native *kringette*. Carstairs was not a man given to philosophy; he was a *groon,* a white hunter. But as he watched the safari winding its way through the rank groves of *bollahulai* he could not dismiss the odd ironies that had cast his lot with Arnold J. Snarf III and his beautiful young wife, Gretchen. A native *kronja* broke up his daydream.

"Massa you come upside threetime white fella him say nogood memsahib allsame walla-walla."

Carstairs paled. He knew what that meant . . .

I wish I did, but the trouble is, I don't speak the language. Almost every day I start a new novel. Some days I write things like "At precisely twelve midnight, Count Snarfini arrived at the door of Number 12. He knocked twice and, as he heard the footsteps, drew the thin blade of polished steel from his sword-cane . . ."; or I write "Hank Snarf was not what you'd call a religious man. And yet the events of May 22, 1882, on the main street of Blood City, were to change his life . . ."; or I write "Julia Moody was not what would normally be called beautiful, and yet there was a certain cast to her face that many men had found attractive. Staring at her now across the bar stool, Mark Grady realized that he loved her—and that it was too late . . ."

After several months of fruitless attempts at producing the novel of the century, I did make one giant leap forward. I discarded my openings and cut to the chase, producing the *endings* of several memorable novels, often working into the night and writing ceaselessly after the manner of Hemingway, Faulkner, Danielle Steel, and others.

The only real trouble was that these endings did not belong to those novels for which I had written beginnings. They belonged to *new* novels. Nonetheless, I am encouraged to quote a few here, and if any budding author has three hundred pages or so to tack on to the opening, he is welcome to these contrived tailpieces.

Here is the ending to a novel of passionate romance and deep tragedy, set on Madagascar, Crete, Majorca, and Hanlan's Point. It is the sort of thing that clicks with the Literary Guild every time:

> All across the bright bay the Prussian blue waters danced as they always had—as they had that morning (was it only last Friday?) when Mark had—but no matter, she must put that out of her mind; it was over, *Finito*.

She knew what she had to do now, knew it as clearly as she knew that her name was not really Julia Hart, that her whole existence had been a sham, a fiction. (Except for the baby, she thought, and a pang of remembrance tore at her heart like a clutching finger: *oh God, the baby!*)

She walked resolutely toward the door, staring straight ahead, marching now with a firm tread, secure in the knowledge of what she must do, not looking back or sideways, turning the knob, blinking as the light, the bright, glittering light, struck at her eyes with the intensity of a whip, seeing once again but not really seeing the picture-postcard houses with their red slate roofs and the picture-postcard people with their grey slate faces, and the bell tower where Robin had first called to her, and the pigeon loft where Derek had made that promise, and the quaint dollhouse of a railway station where Alicia had said goodbye forever.

And as she walked for the last time down that cobbled roadway she felt suddenly a sense of new purpose welling up within her and she knew that she would never be alone again.

There, I've finished it! Bust open the champagne!

It wasn't so hard when I got into the swing of it. The secret is to make the sentences good and long, otherwise it doesn't really sound like a proper novel ending. I wonder what it was that Robin did to her in the bell tower? Well, no matter: put a new sheet in the old typewriter and get on with a new masterpiece. Don't want to get stale, you know:

> "But there's one thing that bothers me about the whole affair, Henshaw, blast it all," I said, tapping the dottle from my pipe. "It was that rum business at the Momalu Bazaar: the old chappie in the scarlet burnoose who made off with the sacred idol's tooth just as Smythe-Wickerbye was about to lay into him with the sultan's scimitar."
>
> "Ah, yes," said Henshaw, casually plucking a cucumber from his Pimm's. "Did I forget to mention that? Rum."
>
> He stared across the jungle for a moment before replying.
>
> "I might as well tell you," he said. "It'll be in the governor's report, anyway. The chap in the burnoose, as you call him, was none other than our old friend, the Hon. Freddie Gross-Patchett, M.P."
>
> And that seemed to end the business for good.

With this kind of ending, you scarcely need a beginning or a middle; it's all there, in the last few paragraphs. Any questions? No? Well, here's another; this is what I call my "in the distance, somewhere, a lark sang" ending:

> Very quietly and gently he laid her on the grass, smoothing out the wet strands of hair that lay vagrant across her pale forehead.

There was nothing more to do. He walked quietly up to the top of the rise, stepping carefully, almost warily, as if fearful of killing some small, living thing with the clumsiness of his tread. Then he sat down on the cool grass and stared out across the valley.

In the distance, somewhere, a lark sang.

It gives you a feeling of accomplishment to achieve this sort of finality; makes you feel like the Hon. Freddie Gross-Patchett, M.P., whoever he is. Noises of all kinds are very good for endings. Take this one:

Suddenly, from nowhere, from everywhere, first softly, then exultantly, he heard the crashing chords of music and the strains of far-off singing. It was the voice of the Heavenly Choir.

Silence, however, is equally good in endings.

He listened attentively, almost wistfully, but there was no answering call. No bird sang; no creature stirred. The very winds were silent and the trees stood like statues. He listened again, half hoping to hear her voice. Nothing. Only the heaving of his empty breast: only the beating of his broken heart.

The above final paragraphs are interchangeable. One more, and then I'll call it a day.

"But, Mike," she said, snuggling closer, "there's just one thing that still puzzles me. How did you know that Alistair Snarf was really a woman in disguise and that he had hidden the secret of the Grootenstein Rubies in Detective-Sergeant Kramer's presentation cuff links after Borg Whelpstein made that abortive attempt on your life with the piranha fish?"

"Simple, baby," I told her. "I simply noticed that the two halves of the broken teacup didn't match up."

"Oh, Mike-doll," she said. "Hold me! Hold me!"

THE END

Six

REMEMBERING THE TWENTIETH-CENTURY CHRISTMAS

A Civil Defence Carol
(To the tune of *It Came Upon the Midnight Clear*)

It came upon the midnight clear,
That glorious sound of old:
Of sirens howling near the earth
To sound the Tocsin-Bold!
"Peace on the Earth! Goodwill to Men!"
The kindly Prime Minister said—
"Those sneaks who wouldn't play games with us
Are acting suspiciously Red."

• • • • • •

A Carol for Sheltered Shut-Ins
(To the tune of *Deck the Hall with Boughs of Holly*)

Deck the wall with steel and mortar
Fa la la la la, la la la la.
Don't forget the purified water
Fa la la la la, la la la la.
Don we now asbestos raiment
Fa la la, la la la, la la la.
Easy terms and no down payment
Fa la la la la, la la la la.

See the blazing town before us
Fa la la la la, la la la la.
Let's give thanks our walls ain't porous
Fa la la la la, la la la la.
Praise we now our earnest labour
Fa la la, la la la, la la la.
Love thy shelter! Shoot thy neighbour!
Fa la la la la, la la la la.

• • • • • •

A Carol for Real Patriots
(To the tune of *O Little Town of Bethlehem*)

O little town of Washington
How still we see thee lie,
Above thy deep and dreamless sleep
The satellites rush by.
Yet in thy bosom struggles
That Truth for which we search.
Our hopes and dreams for all the years
Are resting with John Birch!

• • • • • •

A Carol for Capitalists
(To the tune of *Good Christian Men, Rejoice*)

Good Christian men, rejoice!
With heart and soul and voice!
Give ye heed to what we say:
News! News!
The stock market is up today—
Mr. Khrushchev has raised a row;
Nuclear issues are higher now!
We won't have peace today . . .
We won't have peace today. . . .

• • • • • •

A Carol for UN Delegates
(To the tune of *God Rest You Merry, Gentlemen*)

God rest you, worthy gentlemen:
Let nothing you disarm!
Remember national interest
Still has that certain charm.
Make all your boasts in megatons
And we'll feel no alarm—
O, Tactics of gambit and ploy!
Gambit and ploy!
O, Tactics of gambit and ploy!

• • • • •

A Carol for Mao Tse-tung, Chou En-lai, and Chen Yi
(To the tune of *We Three Kings*)

We three kings of Orient are
Since World War II, we've traversed far
Through forest and weald
And collective field
Following yon Red Star!
Oh Star of Stalin!
Star of Might!
Khrushchev's chicken:
He won't fight!
He's appeasing; we're increasing
In a world no longer white!

• • • • • •

Two Carols for World War Three
(First carol to the tune of *The First Noel*)

When the first bomb fell
The Generals did say
We must retaliate
In a positive way!
In a positive way
So they won't think we're sheep
We've got no other choice
Cause we're in this too deep . . .

CHORUS: *Oh, well! Oh, well!*
             Oh, well! Oh, well!
             There's no way to stop it
             So wot-the-hell?

(Second carol to the tune of *Silent Night*)

Silent Night!
Peaceful Night!
All is calm!
All is bright!
Yonder fires have almost died down
And the wreck that was once a town
Sleeps in Heavenly peace!
Sleeps in Heavenly peace!

The Sixty-five
Days of Christmas

A Carol for November 3

Christmas began last Tuesday
On a bright fall day, with the leaves still
    clinging to the trees.
And no sign of snow—
No sign of any snow,
Unless you count the kind
That's sprayed from aerosol bottles
Onto the imitation Christmas trees
In the department store windows.

Christmas began last Tuesday
Just three days after Halloween,
By which time the big emporiums,
Having disposed of the comic ghosts and candy pumpkins
And having burned all the second-hand witches,
Replaced them with more seasonal symbols:
A reindeer with a crimson nose,
A talking snowman and a terribly cute bear,
Fifty-seven varieties of Santa Claus,
And, here and there, an inconspicuous plastic replica
    of the Christ-child,
Entirely non-denominational.

Christmas began last Tuesday
With corps of workmen spraying rows of fragrant pines
With coats of every hue—
Passion pink, spun gold, and lavender,
Ivory white, lark blue, cerise and silver—
Every colour of the rainbow
With the possible exception of green,
Which has long been out of fashion.

Christmas began last Tuesday
When certain men, from various points East,
Having followed a star
Named Bing Crosby
Into the record shops,
Began to dream of another "White Christmas"
In the guise of a trifle called "Santa Claus Mambo"
And arrived bearing gifts
For the Man Who Has Everything:
Camel saddles imported from Tangier for TV viewing,
Sling beds for toy poodles,
Tubes of bourbon-flavoured toothpaste,
Sets of authentic matchbooks from New York's
     fabulous niteries,
Inflatable dinosaurs, four feet tall,
Thundermugs, lined with genuine mink,
And a partridge in a pear tree.

Christmas began last Tuesday
With the first, faint familiar sounds of "Silent Night,"
Sung by three blonde sisters in an echo chamber,
Stealing across the sleeping town
Courtesy of a sleepless disc jockey
Who does not really believe in nights of silence
And who, every hour on the hour,
Is happy to oblige with Lawrence Welk
Playing his new arrangement of "Jingle Bells,"
Followed by Elvis Presley singing "Adeste Fideles"
In the original Latin.

Christmas began last Tuesday
Because the merchandise was ready.
The composition yule logs were guaranteed fireproof
And so were the plug-in Christmas candles;
The Christmas spirit was guaranteed seventy proof,
Gift-wrapped in decanter bottles
With the Star of Bethlehem on the wrapper;
The new sexified greeting cards were guaranteed
    tasteproof,
Complete with buxom girls inviting you
To have a ball at Christmas,
And plenty of space for your name in 18-karat gold.

Christmas began last Tuesday
And will continue for the duration,
Plodding steadily onward
Through a calendarful of shopping days,

And a gaggle of office parties,
And a surfeit of constabulary warnings;
Moving right past Boxing Day and into the
    Happy New Year
Until, on Tuesday, January 8, it will officially end
With the first of the post-Christmas sales;
At which time, the gifts selected at the last frantic moment
For the man who has everything but myrrh and frankincense,
May be returned at the first possible moment by his wife
Who, if she fancies, can buy for half-price, reduced to clear,
In the bargain basements of a score of Honest Edifices,
A mile and a half of slightly tarnished tinsel,
Which may be stored away in case Christmas should ever
    come around again.

So then, when it is finally over and done with—
The sixty-five days of Christmas—
And there are three hundred days remaining
Before Christmas begins again,
And people look back and ask themselves:
"What kind of day was it?"
The answer will have to be:
"A day like all days."
For the sad fact is that nobody can quite remember
    any more
Exactly which, of all the Christmas Days,
Was the one marked on the calendar
As December the twenty-fifth.

Dear Mr. Eaton:
What's a Knurled
Centre Pin?

"RANCH WAGON" PEDAL AUTO. *Features include battery-operated headlights, smooth-running chain drive and modern, low styling. All-steel body is smart, two-tone enamel finish. Plated grills and hubcaps; spring-type radio aerial. Sturdy metal seat with extra space at rear; handrails. Speedy, easy-to-pedal chain drive to rear wheels; ball-bearing pedal cranks and ball bearings in rear axle for smooth operation. Seven-and-a-half-inch disk wheels roll on nylon bearings, have thick rubber tires. For children up to six years of age. About 41 3/4 inches long, 15 inches wide. 027-G-1084.*

Mr. John David Eaton, President
Eaton's of Canada
Yonge and Queen Streets
Toronto

DEAR MR. EATON:
It is three o'clock on Christmas morning and I thought I would just take time off from assembling your Ranch Wagon Pedal Auto (027-G-1084) to drop you a note.

I have been working steadily on this auto since Christmas Eve, Mr. Eaton, and at this point I am a little beat. I spent most of Christmas Eve with pipe wrench and screwdriver trying to put this device together. It is exhilarating work, no doubt, but I am not cut out for it.

Now I know you are a big and important businessman with a great deal on your mind, and I do not wish to say anything that might be considered inflammatory. I realize that you are an upright citizen, and I understand, from my reading of the papers, that you periodically make large contributions to the United Way. So I will be temperate in this letter, Mr. Eaton.

It's just that every time I try to attach the side-rail assembly (5725) to pal nut (b) I have an uncontrollable urge to strangle you.

Strangling, I might add, is far too good for the genius who drew up the set of diagrams that accompanies the lengthy list of instructions that is attached to the kit of 367 separate parts (a rough guess) that I am required to put together at 10:30 p.m. on Christmas Eve in time for Santa to drop this Ranch Wagon Chain-O-Matic Pedal Automobile down the chimney.

Where do you get your engineers, anyway, Eaton—from the White Sands Proving Grounds? At the moment I am staring fixedly at the diagrammatic schematic cross-section mechanical drawing that accompanies the set of plans marked "Assembly of Steering wheel." If I had a Ph.D. from M.I.T. I might just be able to get this thing together, but as matters stand, I am a little puzzled.

Before I get this auto off the launching pad I have to have one tiny piece of information about the steering wheel, and I would appreciate your sending it along by return mail.

Instruction No. 265A says, and I quote: "Drive 7/8 inch long knurled centre pin (8) in hole and slide bracket (7) back up over pin (8)."

What do you use for this job—a pile-driver?

I've been trying for seven hours, with scarcely any time off for food or brandy, to drive that knurled centre pin into that hole. I have hammered it with crescent wrenches, the flat ends of axes, wooden mallets, claw hammers and even a meat tenderizer, and outside of busting several wooden handles, I have got absolutely nowhere.

I haven't worked so fruitlessly since that certain Black Friday, years ago, when I tried to put together the combination swing, teeter-totter, and home gymnast set, which I notice you are still callously listing in your summer catalogue.

I have, for the moment, left off tampering with the 7/8-inch knurled centre pin (8) and have gone back to General Instruction No. 5.

To attach rear axle assembly, remove tape from chain. Place flat side of rear arch assembly on a flat surface to the rear of the housing, withdraw axle from one end of assembly so that you can slip chain over the rear axle sprocket and replace axle in bearing. (Be sure that chain is around both the front and rear sprocket.) Housing support brace will be on the inside of the rear arch assembly.

I wish I'd written that. It has such a fine authoritative ring. It bespeaks a man to whom housing support braces and rear arch assemblies are household words. I can see him coming home at night, having replaced several axles in their bearings, all aglow with the satisfaction of having composed that paragraph. "Wait till the peasants read that!" you can hear him saying.

"Housing support brace will be on the inside of the rear arch assembly." Get that prose! Beside it some of Joyce's more obscure stream-of-consciousness paragraphs are amber-clear. Why, it makes a Lasker chess problem seem like a game of Old Maid!

I enclose a stamped, self-addressed envelope, Mr. Eaton, and all I want to know is: how do you tell the inside of a rear arch assembly from the *outside* of a rear arch assembly? No doubt you have a few old arch assemblies (rear and front) kicking around your basement, so let me in on the secret.

Mr. Eaton, I had the naïve idea when I bought this auto that all I had to do was open the package and it would roll out and over to the Christmas tree. I did not understand that, for no extra charge, I was to get a combined kid's toy auto and father's do-it-yourself kit.

Well, as far as I am concerned, this has become a do-yourself-in kit.

Of course, after my really terrifying experience with your Easy-to-Assemble Garden Swing, your patented Put-Together Doll's House, and your Knock-Down All-Plastic Rocking Horse, I should have known better.

Tomorrow I plan to order your 053-T-5813 "Better Home" Tool Kit (group of 27 matched Handyman tools in metal cabinet 16" x 26") and turn the whole problem over to the three-year-old boy for whom this auto was intended. Let him grapple with it.

Meanwhile, there is only one more General Instruction I intend to follow—No. 14: "Lubricate all moving parts from time to time for easier operation."

I presume that means me. I only have a few moving parts left, Mr. Eaton, but they can stand lubrication.

Hoping you and your family are well, I am,

Your humble and obedient customer,

Dissident Thoughts on
Our Best-Known Carol

"Santa Claus Is Comin' to Town" was written in 1934 as a "novelty foxtrot" and has, since then, become an enduring Christmas symbol—like Noma lights and The Man Who Has Everything. The tune is innocuous enough, the lyrics less so:

You better watch out; you better not cry—
Better not pout, I'm telling you why:
Santa Claus is comin' to town!

There is a chorus for the Twentieth Century! Bottle up your tears, kiddies; sublimate your emotions or Santa will get you! The sentiment is not one that will appeal, I am afraid, to a modern behaviouralist. The theory has long been held that a certain amount of tears and some mercurial pouting are natural to all small children, and that to deny them this normal expression of emotion in their formative years is to warp their personalities in later life.

Dr. Carl Williams, one of the best-known psychologists of our time, had this to say on the subject: "It's a dreadful affair, really. Or it would be if the kids paid any attention to the words. If they looked at those lines with adult logic they'd be completely shattered.

"To impose on a small child the kind of taboo that crying is somehow a bad thing is not only nonsense—it's also dangerous nonsense. I suspect that a great deal of the anxiety, the insecurity and the pathetic desire to please and placate at all costs that one finds in some disturbed adults, derives from this kind of parental attitude toward children."

To try to bottle up the tears of a child, in short, is like trying to hold down the lid of a bubbling kettle.

> *He's making a list and checking it twice,*
> *Gonna find out who's naughty and nice,*
> *Santa Claus is comin' to town.*

The idea of dividing children, as in a TV serial, into two opposing groups of Good and Bad Guys is a popular one, I suppose, since everything these days seems to be pigeon-holed in terms of Black and White. But the idea, as expressed in these lyrics, of bribing the Good Guys with presents and punishing the Bad Guys by withdrawing gifts, is one that I find personally horrifying.

Yet all over town this joyous Yule there will be parents whispering to children, "Unless you're good, Santa Claus won't bring you anything for Christmas!" As most parents won't have the stomach to carry out this threat, the warning only makes liars out of them in their kids' eyes. But, apart from this, it is, as Dr. Williams has remarked, "a sort of bargain basement form of discipline." It works—but at what a cost!

What the song really says is *Don't be naughty or you won't be loved*, and that's as good a way of shattering a child's emotional makeup as the psychologists know.

Again, Dr. Williams: "The only thing a mother has to sell is the economic and emotional security that she gives to a child. Children are obviously insecure, anyway, and so we parents have them by the short hairs. If a mother says: 'My love is up for sale; I'll take it away if you don't do what I say,' she is using the most powerful coercive there is. It's the easy way out, all right—but it's the worst way."

Jesus Christ, with whom this season was once intimately associated, was the first man to come up with the novel proposition that love ought to be extended to everybody—Bad Guys, Good Guys, beggar men, thieves, and even those awful Samaritans. How ironic that the Christian image of the compassionate Man should have been replaced by that of the villainous Claus, sneaking about from house-top to house-top with his list in his hand, checking it twice like an FBI agent, crossing off a name here, denying a gift there (to a child who cries), cutting off the pension of a moppet who has been Naughty, slipping a small bit of payola to another who has been Nice, and masquerading all the time as a kindly old party, shouting *Ho! Ho! Ho!* while he pats little children on the head like a politician and holds them still long enough for the full-colour photograph to be taken by the hidden camera for three bucks a throw.

He sees you while you're sleeping,
He knows when you're awake,
He knows when you've been bad or good,
So be good for goodness sake!

Now we are getting to the crux of the matter. There is no escape from this Orwellian Santa, with his X-ray eyes and his terrible List. The darkest closet will not conceal the sobbing child when Big Brother is on the job; the smallest pout cannot pass unnoticed.

S. CLAUS
IS WATCHING YOU

Seven

THE OFTEN LIVELY ARTS

The Art of Chinese Foodmanship

In his admirable studies of Gamesmanship, Lifemanship and One-Upmanship, Mr. Stephen Potter has left one field entirely unexplored. It is a pity, since it offers such a rich and rewarding study for the Advanced Lifeman.

I refer, of course, to Chinese Foodmanship, or the Art of Eating Noodles Without Ever Ordering Chow Mein. I suspect the reason for this is that the Chinese food in England is usually execrable—almost as bad, indeed, as it is in China. In such surroundings the Egg Foo Yong ploy or the Tay Dop Voy gambit is hardly effective.

I have been a Chinese Foodman now since the age of nineteen and in recent times have seldom been bested at the art. I must admit to being severely shaken several years back when R. Allen of *Maclean's*, in a brilliant gambit, ordered an entire meal in the Chinese language. It developed that he had cornered a Lichee Gardens menu and had spent weeks phonetically committing it to memory.

Allen has also given his name to the historic *Allen Response to the Chopstick Ploy.* This is, of course, one of the basic ploys in Chinese Foodmanship and until the invention of the Allen Response, dextrous chopstick play was considered mandatory for those wishing to be one-up.

The Allen response is childishly simple:

ALLEN *(politely)*: Still using chopsticks, I see?
CHINESE FOODMAN: Still?

ALLEN *(warmly)*: I got a great kick out of them, too, when I was a kid.

(Chinese Foodman stares glumly at chopsticks.)

ALLEN *(takes him by the arm)*: No! No! Please don't be embarrassed. I know a lot of people think it's an affectation, but I still remember the kick I got out of my first fumbling attempts to handle them. Please—go on; I like to watch you.

In this brilliant fashion, Allen, who is absolutely incapable of using chopsticks, makes himself a master of the situation and can move quickly into the *Do You Mind If I Order?* gambit with its accompanying counterploys. If the gambit is handled correctly the novice can usually be manoeuvred into paying the bill in a desperate attempt to regain some one-upmanship.

CHINESE FOODMAN: Look, do you mind if I order? I know the menu rather well.

NOVICE: Please do.

CHINESE FOODMAN: What do you fancy?

The alert novice, if he is on his toes, will now suggest a really obscure dish, using the Chinese terms in an effort to best his opponent. The response here is standard:

CHINESE FOODMAN: M-m-m-m. I shouldn't try that here if I were you; I've had it a couple of times and it tends to be a bit on the crisp side. Might I suggest the Lo Har Wop

Tee? They do it superbly here; in my opinion, it rivals Ho Mein's in 'Frisco.

Alternately, a real novice may mumble something about "chicken chow mein." Once this awful phrase is out, he is at the mercy of the practised Chinese Foodman. The most effective attitude here is one of polite and friendly condescension rather than straight scorn.

CHINESE FOODMAN: Chicken chow mein, eh? *(Chuckles indulgently.)* Well, well, well! If that's what you want, that's what you shall have! I'll see if I can get a single portion.

NOVICE: What's wrong? I thought that's what everybody had.

CHINESE FOODMAN *(very slowly and patiently but good-humouredly)*: Now there's nothing wrong at all. Lots of people order chow mein, especially when they're learning. There's nothing at all to be ashamed of. It's a perfectly good dish even though it's something the Chinese themselves wouldn't look twice at.

NOVICE: Look? Please? I just didn't know. Cancel the chow mein. You order.

CHINESE FOODMAN: Certainly not! You stick to your guns. Waiter *(Loudly)*! Here's a man who wants chow mein!

If he is certain that his opponent is not practised in the Allen Response, an alert Chinese Foodman can do a great deal with the actual mechanics of eating. The first thing to do is order a bowl rather than a plate and fill it with steamed rice. Then make a great fetish of eating "Chinese-style" by selecting tidbits from the common dishes, dipping them into the rice and passing them, via the chopsticks, to the mouth. A practised chopstick man is not only one-up on his opponent by virtue of this mumbo-jumbo but he can usually get three times as much to eat.

For Foodmen less practised with chopsticks the method can be made even more effective by raising the bowl to the mouth, bending slightly forward, and shovelling the food in with the chopsticks. You will be surprised how really Oriental this makes you look.

I warn you, however, that there is a response to this gambit that seasoned Foodmen use:

SEASONED CHINESE FOODMAN *(chuckling)*: Coolie-style, eh?

NOVICE: *Coolie* style?

S.C.F.: The position you're affecting is perfectly authentic, but I'm afraid it would be considered beneath contempt in any sophisticated Chinese home. But you go ahead; I get a kick out of watching you do that.

In Toronto there is an élite of Chinese Foodmen composed of those of us who once ate at a little place known as 22A Elizabeth Street that has since been demolished. It is useful in besting a particularly knowing opponent.

OPPONENT: Look, I want you to try the won ton here. They do it superbly. In my opinion, it's the best this side of Gar Choy's in 'Frisco.

CHINESE FOODMAN: H-m-m-m. Not bad. I wish, though, you could have tried the won ton they used to serve in 22A. It was the real thing. But that would be before your time.

Of course, 22A was a miserable place with no decor and drab oilcloth-covered tables. True Chinese Foodmen always try to lure their opponents into such hovels. When taken to a sumptuous restaurant complete with orchestra and murals, the most effective gambit is to mention Ho Gee's hole-in-the-wall down the street.

CHINESE FOODMAN: Of course, the decor here is lovely, but for real, authentic Chinese food, give me Ho Gee's. That's where the Chinese themselves eat. I admit the surroundings aren't up to much, but they make a Gar Whop Chee there that melts in your mouth.

You were asking about the Egg Foo Yong ploy mentioned at the outset? Well, expert Chinese Foodmen know that real Egg Foo Yong can be cooked three ways: light, medium or well-done. There's a little place on Dundas Street that does it this way. Try their bean-cake soup while you're at it. The decor isn't much, but the cuisine is the best I've had this side of Chee Loy Duck's in 'Frisco.

Recognizing Three
National Heros

It is now generally understood that the old movies shown on television are the handiwork of J. Alistair McGraw. But it is only comparatively recently that McGraw's great contribution to the industry has been acknowledged. For years he worked in obscurity, making old movies in rented barns and aircraft hangars, unknown and unheralded by the public who enjoyed his handiwork. That was all right with McGraw; he wanted it that way.

Of course, originally, old movies actually *were* "old." Even as late as 1959 most of the old movies seen on television were made in the 1930s and 1940s. It was about this period that McGraw got his great idea.

He realized that the stock of old movies was rapidly becoming depleted. Yet every survey showed that old movies were the most popular programs on the air. *The Smiling Lieutenant* with Claudette Colbert, made in 1931, could even outdraw such top shows as *Cannonball, Live a Borrowed Life*, etc.

That's when McGraw decided to form his own company to manufacture new old movies. Not only were old movies cheaper to make than new movies but the public obviously preferred them. The dialogue could be insincere, the characterizations flabby, the film quality murky, the direction feeble, and the stars faded; the public liked it that way.

In their declining years, the stars (Joan Blondell, George Raft, Andrea Leeds, Rochelle Hudson, Nat Pendleton, Vera Ralston, Alice Faye, Richard Arlen, Frank McHugh and many others) were glad to get work again, and McGraw's product was indistinguishable from the real McCoy. The titles and plots were such that the public was certain it had seen the movies before: *Rainbow on My Knee, It Happened Next Thursday, October's Children, Footlights of 1933, Desperate Message,* etc. The element of nostalgia was ever-present.

McGraw made a fortune but remained in obscurity. Only now is he getting the recognition he deserves. A plaque to his memory will be unveiled next Friday at 3 p.m. in the lobby of Channel 13 in Hamilton, and a short memorial program will be presented at two o'clock the next morning following the Late Show. Van Johnson and Cyd Charisse are flying in for the affair.

• • • • • •

The contribution made by Roland Frobisher to the economic system of North America deserves more notice than it has hitherto received. Frobisher, almost single-handedly, has prevented an imminent depression. Thanks to him, a slump has been postponed for at least a generation.

It was Frobisher who completely revised the instalment system, which he once described as "a creaky nineteenth-century vehicle unsuited for the atomic era."

Back in 1959, Frobisher was an appliance salesman; he sold refrigerators, TV sets, kitchen ranges, electric egg frothers and such. Everything was *One Third Down, Twelve Months to Pay* at first, but later as competition got tougher it was *Ten Percent Down, Two Years to Pay*, and later on it became *Nothing Down, Five Years to Pay.*

Still, Frobisher felt, this wasn't really enough. His first

tentative fumbling toward the new-type instalment system came when he put up a sign in his window that shook his competitors to the marrow: *Nothing Down, A LIFETIME TO PAY*. By this ingenious system, customers could still be paying for a refrigerator after it had worn out and had been replaced by a new one. The idea caught on like wildfire. Still, Frobisher was not satisfied.

The great idea came to him while he lay on the deck of his palatial yacht, moored off the Spanish coast. He took his private plane back to his appliance store immediately. The following day he took double-truck ads in all the papers and spot announcements on the better radio stations (such as CKFH). Their slogan: *Nothing Down: Nothing to Pay; YOUR CHILDREN PAY!*

This was Frobisher's lasting accomplishment. By visiting the purchases of the fathers on to the next generation he induced the greatest spending spree in North America's history. Everybody had everything they wanted and everybody was rich. Instalments did not start until the children became of age, and legal documents, prepared by Frobisher's battery of high-priced lawyers, made sure that they would carry out their parents' obligations.

It may be a bit tough on the future generation but, as Frobisher says, we'll all be dead and gone by then.

● ● ● ● ● ●

Has Reginald deB. Brewster ever been given the credit he deserves for revolutionizing the radio business? Do people ever remember what radio was like in the days before Brewster took over? I doubt it.

Well, it was anarchy. You turned on a radio station and you never knew what you were going to get. One station would have music playing one minute, the news the next and then some woman talking. Sometimes *all* the stations would have exactly the same thing on, like they'd all have the news on at noon, but at 12:15 you couldn't get any news. Or every single one, sometimes, would be playing *Teen-Age Cha-Cha*.

If you wanted to get Number Three on the Hit Parade, for instance, you just couldn't get it automatically by turning on the radio—not unless you waited for quite a while. That's how it was in those days, and don't think there weren't complaints.

Then along came Reginald deB. Brewster with his great idea. It was he who realized that radio stations had become so numerous, and radio sets so sensitive, that almost everybody could tune in on twelve different stations. Plenty of people knew this, but Brewster was the only one to sense the possibilities.

For his pilot project he simply bought up twelve radio stations to test his idea. It was an instantaneous success. Ten of the stations simply played the ten top tunes on the hit parade interspersed with commercials. That is to say, the first station played No. 1 on the Hit Parade over and over again all day long; the second station played No. 2, etc. The eleventh station gave the news from the Canadian Press ticker over and over again, and the twelfth station kept giving weather announcements (interspersed, of course, with commercials) over and over again. For the listener it was pie: you could always get the Top Ten or the weather or the news by turning to a specific station. As this was all that people wanted, anyway, it made it very cheap to run radio stations. You didn't have to hire disc jockeys, political commentators, drama producers, musicians or anybody. To operate twelve stations all you needed was one announcer, ten records and the Canadian Press wire service. Oh, yes, and a man to count the money.

Reginald deB. Brewster became immensely wealthy as a result of what became known as "chain-store" broadcasting. But it wasn't wealth he wanted so much as recognition, and finally he got that, too. The papers began to refer to him as "the Roy Thomson of radio."

Recycling an Old TV
Hit—Canadian Style

It is a puzzlement that the grand old CBC, often bereft of bright new ideas, doesn't take a leaf from Hollywood and recycle old television shows to make them look brand new. There are many former hits that lend themselves to such treatment. I'm thinking especially of a big-budget program produced in the early days of television and entitled *The Big Party*. In true-blue Canadian hands this could be a real gasser.

It seems childishly simple to produce. In one memorable show they just put a few cameras in the home of the screen star Greer Garson, and we viewers sort of peeped in while she held one of her gay, spontaneous parties. A few of the neighbours dropped in—neighbours like Martha Raye, Walter Slezak, Elaine May, Mike Nichols, Peter Lind Hayes, Mary Healy, Sal Mineo—and sat around chatting and performing little acts, which they seemed to do very expertly.

Well, I'm suggesting the CBC add to its all-Canadian content by producing its own party. Since it's an all-Canadian party, however, a few changes will have to be made.

The party begins at 9:30, see, which means that for the first hour and a half all the viewers will see is a black living room. We have a rule in this country that if you call a party for 9:30 you really mean eleven o'clock. Sometimes the host and hostess don't even get there until eleven. They've been at one of those five- to seven-o'clock cocktail affairs that begin at eight and go on to 10:30.

Just to enliven proceedings, we might show a variation on the theme: The Couple That Arrives on Time.

HOSTESS: Good heavens, there's the doorbell; somebody's here! Quick, the dishes! Chuck all that loose junk in the broom closet! Kick those toys under the sofa! You go. I'm in my slip.

HOST: I'm in my overalls. *(He hitches up his pants and answers the door, while the hostess flees to the bathroom.)*

MALE GUEST: I'm afraid we're a bit early.

HOST: Certainly not. I just checked the clock and you're exactly on time.

FEMALE GUEST: I told George we were too early, but he always insists on being prompt. When we saw the lights weren't on we drove around the block several times, but George just had to come in.

MALE GUEST: Say, I didn't realize this was a masquerade party.

HOST: Oh, *these*! Just some old rags I threw on. I just like to be comfortable, that's all.

FEMALE GUEST: I hope we haven't thrown you folks off schedule by arriving early.

HOST: Nonsense! Why, I was just saying to Madge, if there's one thing I hate it's people who aren't prompt! Come on in; as soon as I get these dishes washed I'll pour you a drink.

Now when the rest of the guests get there, we've got to make another fundamental Canadian change. At Greer

Garson's party, everybody mixed it up. We're going to play it for real on the good old CBC. As soon as the coats are off, all the women will go over and sit down on the sofa. They will stay there all night without moving. All the men will go out into the kitchen.

Periodically, the hostess will come into the kitchen and try to drag some men out. She will say things like "How about you fellows joining the party?" or "Come on, boys, let's circulate." The men will stay in the kitchen.

She will suggest games like charades, musical chairs, Twenty Questions, etc., and several of the women will actually start to play these games. The men will stay in the kitchen.

One of the features of the Big Party that intrigued me was the ease with which people performed party tricks. Like somebody would say, "Hey, Greer, why don't you do the death scene from *Camille*?" Instantly Greer would do the death scene from *Camille*. Or somebody would say, "Hey, Peter Lind Hayes and Mary Healy, how about performing one of your famous nightclub acts?" And Peter Lind Hayes and Mary Healy would comply instantly.

Well, if we're to maintain 55 percent Canadian content, we'll have to change the script a bit:

GUEST: Hey, let's get good old Ken to tell his rickshaw story!

ALL GUESTS *(except Mrs. Ken)*: Yes, yes! Ken's rickshaw story! He does it so well! Doesn't he do it well? Come on, Ken, boy! Tell your rickshaw story!

KEN: Don't feel like telling the rickshaw story.

3RD GUEST: Give him a coupla drinks. He only tells it after a coupla drinks.

KEN: I might tell it after a coupla drinks.

MRS. KEN: Ken, do you think you should?

Well, by the time Ken has a coupla drinks, the hostess announces supper is ready. This is always a delicate business as several of the men obstinately refuse to eat, saying, no thanks, they'll just nurse another rye. We get several shots of wives coaxing husbands to eat, actually feeding them forkfuls of provender without much success.

After that, just as Ken is about to tell the rickshaw story, a rather frail woman stands up and in a piercing whisper says she hopes she's not breaking anything up, but they have a teenage babysitter at home and they just mustn't be late.

At this everybody stands up and starts climbing into coats. The hostess begins to run from one couple to another, saying please don't go yet, it's so early and things are beginning to liven up, and besides Ken is going to tell his rickshaw story.

By this time everybody is halfway out the door and the host, his jacket off and tie loosened, is padding softly toward the den when one guest says okay, he wouldn't mind having just one more.

WIFE: Horace! You're keeping them up.

HORACE: You shut up! If you don't like it, go out and sit in the car.

WIFE: I can't do anything with him when he gets this way.

You're sure we're not keeping you up?

HOST: No! No! We were just hoping someone would stay. I only put on these pyjamas because I got tired of the overalls.

And so we sign off, credits and titles supered over the scene as Horace talks his head off and our host and hostess slowly drift off to dreamland on the chesterfield. Another All-Canadian Party has stumbled to its close.

When I Am Old
and Weary I Plan
to Open A Dream Café

MANAGER: *The soup, Gaston—has it been cooled suffi-ciently?*

WAITER: *I just this moment dropped a lump of ice into the plate, sir. It has the added advantage of giving the dish that watery consistency for which we are famous.*

MANAGER: *The french-fried potatoes are suitably limp?*

WAITER: *They have been lying around for half an hour, slowly limping.*

MANAGER: *Excellent! I see they are beginning to wrinkle. Now, how about the roast beef?*

WAITER: *It has been smothered under a heavy mass of our special gravy. No one will ever see it again.*

MANAGER: *Capital! Everything seems to be in order. You may serve the customer. Who did you say he was?*

WAITER: *Chap making a survey of the average Canadian restaurant. Name of Berton. He looks a bit haggard . . .*

••••••

The Canadian Tourist Association has been indulging in some honest self-examination regarding hotel and restaurant facilities in this country. The consensus is that we just aren't in the same league as the United States. As far as the restaurants are concerned, I'm obliged to agree.

I do not mean our top-grade restaurants. These are as good as anything south of the border. I don't mean our bottom-grade restaurants, either. These are no worse than their U.S.

counterparts. What I'm talking about is the thick stratum of "average" places.

If I had one criticism to make of the average medium-priced Canadian restaurant I would say that the managers did not pay as much attention to small details as the Americans do. It is not the main dishes that bother me so much as the side dishes: the vegetables, salads, soups, sauces and condiments. Quite often they are simply appalling.

I have often thought that when I am forced to retire to some quiet hamlet, I might easily make ends meet as proprietor of a small eating place on the main street. I will call it the Queen's Café, or the Royal or perhaps the Princess Tea Room—something suitably Canadian. There I will pass my declining years, trying to feed people properly. It is only a daydream, I suppose, but a harmless one.

In my restaurant, a great deal of attention will be paid to soups. All soups will be served in deep bowls, and they will be so hot that warning signs to this effect will be erected next to the WATCH YOUR COAT placards. That staple of the "average" Canadian restaurant, navy bean soup, will never be served. But we will have such thick soups as New England clam chowder and French-Canadian pea. Croutons, toasted crisp in chicken fat, will be served with all thick soups. These, too, will be hot enough to make a satisfactory sizzling sound when dropped into the steaming tureen. No tinned soups will be served, but we will have a good chicken consommé on hand at all times, and twice weekly we will have rich beef tea made from beef heart.

In my restaurant we will treat vegetables with the respect

they deserve. Any man who mixes carrots and peas together in one dish will get a skewer in his gizzard. Carrots will be banned entirely, except in the early summer when they are young and sweet. Beets also will be served only in season, and always with their greens. Cabbage will be boiled with corned beef or ham but otherwise will be scalloped with bread crumbs and cheese. Tinned peas will be cooked in a consommé to which small pieces of bacon and onion have been added. Spinach will never be offered to a customer without a grating of hard-boiled egg on top.

We will have fried, hash brown and french-fried potatoes on every menu. French-fried potatoes will be cut small and neat, never in large lumps. If a customer has to take two bites to eat one french-fried potato, the chef himself will be french fried. They will be crisped to a deep golden brown like the toast. When eaten they will make a suitably crunchy sound under the impress of the teeth, but within they will remain as light and fluffy as gossamer.

The hash brown potatoes will be properly hashed and properly browned. They will be shredded to the size of match sticks, woven into a small mattress, dropped into a hot, cast iron pan alive with spattering oil and given an enviable crust. The home-fried potatoes will be chopped into bite-sized morsels (from firm, pre-cooked potatoes) and given individual attention by the chef. They should be crusty on the outside but laughing on the inside with the hot succulence of youth.

Coleslaw in my restaurant will be a dish in itself. It will be shredded, not chopped, and as crisp as an Arctic afternoon.

Brainstorming sessions will be held weekly to discuss the quality of the marinade.

We will institute a firm rule about Southern-Fried Chicken in my restaurant: at least 65 percent of this staple dish must actually consist of chicken. This is about 20 percent higher than many restaurants allow, but I do not think it is too high a goal to aim at. After all, it still permits the blacksmith at the griddle plenty of leeway when dousing the naked bird with its thick coat of library paste. On second thought, let's be daring and insist that at least 70 percent of the fried chicken actually consist of chicken and not batter. If this be treason, eat at Joe's.

Ketchup and steak sauces will not be allowed in my restaurant. Any customer asking for ketchup will be forcibly removed by my assistant, Whipper Billy Watson, and directed to the Acme Bar & Grill ("Home of Good Eats") down the street. Special relishes and pickles, made to our own formula, will be at every table, however. No customer will have to ask for them.

The following desserts will be banned: rice pudding, Jell-O, stewed prunes, wet custard and pies with shiny tops. Pies with crumbly tops made from fresh fruits will be served in season. There will be no cornstarch in the pie filling, and customers will be warned to protect themselves when the pies are opened since the fragrant juices will spurt from the lacerated crust like the hot blood of a newly sacrificed virgin.

Tea will be made in individual heated pots without benefit of tissue paper or gauze. It will be made, in short, as the English make it in the belief that the English know more about making tea than we do. Coffee will be made in Silex-es (for breakfast coffee) and in small French drip pots (for dinner coffee) but never in great metal vats with pipes down the side.

And the printed menus will be very simple. As all eggs will be country-fresh, all vegetables garden-pure, and all but-ter made in a creamery, we will not feel it necessary to call attention to it on the bill of fare.

That's how it will be at my restaurant. I can hardly wait to go broke.

News Items from the World of Fashion

Berton announces "Barrel Look"
Famous Designer Shocks Fashion World

PARIS, Feb. 19 (Special)—Pierre Berton, the "enfant terrible" of the Parisian fashion world, shook his fellow-designers to the core today when he unveiled his sensational new "barrel look" at the annual spring showings in his world-famous salon.

Breaking sharply with tradition, M. Berton has concealed all semblance of the female curves behind an all-embracing barrel-shaped garment.

Gasps of awe and mingled hisses greeted the chic models as they strode down the ramp displaying the new Berton creations. Some of the garments, according to observers, seemed to have been made of actual wooden staves held together with a series of simple iron rings.

Asked what fabrics predominate in the new style, M. Berton replied: "We only use the finest white oak."

● ● ● ● ● ●

"Barrel Look" leaves Toronto cold
Won't Adopt Berton Fad, Say Local Lovelies

Toronto women today turned their thumbs unanimously down on Paris couturier Pierre Berton's controversial "barrel look" for the coming year. Few women questioned had anything but contempt for the new styles.

"Canadian women just won't wear barrels," said Mme Jean Chrétien. "Like my husband, I prefer the old looks."

"I can't speak for the Canadian people, but personally I'm indifferent to the barrel look," said lovely TV star Dini Petty.

"Hide what we've got under a barrel? He must think we're all crazy," scoffed radio star Avril Benoit.

"They certainly aren't getting me into a barrel," declared lovely bank executive A.M. Sten.

(Similar comments by Dolly Parton, Raquel Welch, Kim Campbell, and Shelley Winters can be found on page 3).

• • • • • •

Basic insecurities of era
seen in newest barrel fad

LONDON, April 19 (AP)—In seeking to hide their feminine charms by the wearing of barrel-shaped garments, today's women are only pointing up the basic insecurities of the age in which they live, James Laver, the British Museum's expert on fashions, stated today.

"All down through the ages there have been periods when women sought to conceal their charms from men," Mr. Laver pointed out. "It is no coincidence that these were periods of either great tension or great calm."

The museum expert added that by wearing barrels designed by famed Paris couturier Pierre Berton women were only seeking to "erect a wall between themselves and a world they cannot understand."

"All through history the barrel has been a kind of symbol," Mr. Laver explained.

• • • • • •

Local stave factory
back in business

By J.R. "Jack" Carstairs

(Assoc. Editor, Grebesville Courier-Times-Express)

A street dance will be held at Main and Queen at 7 o'clock sharp this evening to celebrate the re-opening of the Grebesville Stave Factory, closed since 1923, as announced last night by L. Jason Snood.

Interviewed by the *Courier-Times-Express* regarding the sudden boom in business, it was learned that the barrel seems to have come into its own again.

"Suddenly," said Mr. Snood, "the world seems to have grown barrel-conscious."

No examples of the new Barrel Look have yet appeared on Grebesville streets, and it is to be hoped that this "high fashion" will be confined to the larger centres, such as Barrie, where it belongs.

• • • • • •

"What's wrong with barrels?"
—Pamela Anderson,
bosomy star,
touts newest Fashion "Look"

HOLLYWOOD, June 22 (UPI)—Busty Pamela Anderson hopped aboard the barrel bandwagon today with the announcement that a little "provocative concealment" is just what the nation needs.

Posing in a shoulder-to-knee pink barrel with rhinestone-studded hoops, Miss Anderson insisted that the new style added to the imagination.

"The days of bare essentials are gone," she said. "What really interests men is what they *don't* see."

Miss Anderson added that the barrel look was catching on with women because it was the most practical to come along for many years. "It's extremely comfortable and especially cool in the summer," she said. "With the average woman that's what really counts."

• • • • • •

Husband shot, wife held

GREBESVILLE, Aug 22 (Special)—Mrs. Elsie Snood was charged here today with attempted murder of her husband after a dispute over the Barrel Look.

Police said Mrs. Snood shot her husband when he refused her funds to purchase the new fashion.

Police said Mrs. Snood said that every other woman in town had a barrel and she felt "left out."

Police said Mrs. Snood said her husband said that was no reason to act like an idiot.

"So I picked up a nearby rifle and aimed between his eyes," police said a neighbour said Mrs. Snood said.

Mr. Snood is in Grebesville Memorial Hospital recovering from a bullet wound in the ankle.

• • • • • •

Famous designer shocks fashion world

PARIS, Sept. 2 (Special)—Pierre Berton, the "enfant terrible" of the Parisian fashion world, shook his fellow-designers to the core today when he unveiled his sensational new "sarong look" at the annual fall showings in his world-famous salon. "The barrel is out," he said.

Following the showing, the Parisian fashion world was in an uproar, with rival camps arguing the merits of the bold new designs. Most experts seemed to agree with the opinions of Emilee van der Krog, famed New York fashion consultant, who stated flatly that "American women will never wear sarongs."

Perry Mason and the Case of the Dapper Detective

In this dream, see, I am the world's greatest criminal lawyer, fighting tooth and nail for my client. At the moment I am conducting a brilliant and penetrating examination of one of the prosecution witnesses. The wretch is cringing in the box under the harsh light of my questioning. His name is Perry Mason.

ME: Now, Mr. Mason, I think it's time we examined your sources of income.

MASON: I have nothing to hide. My income consists entirely of legal fees received from clients.

ME (*sneering*): Your legal fees! Ha! Since when, Mason, have you ever accepted a legal fee from a client?

MASON: Now just a minute—in *The Case of the Pitiful Prowler*, I—

ME (*reading from a document*): You accepted just thirty-seven cents, according to this TV script I have here.

MASON: Well, she needed my help.

ME: Exactly! They all need your help! And you always take their case! And you never ask for money because they never have money? Yet you have an enormous office, roughly the size of the ballroom at the Four Seasons, and a flashy modern desk and a flashy modern secretary and you have at your beck and call at all times the Paul Drake Detective Agency—

HAMILTON BURGER: Objection, your honour! I really do not see what this recital of Mr. Mason's personal effects has to do with the case at hand . . .

ME: If it please the court, I intend to show that the witness Mason at no time acts like a real grasping lawyer. This line of questioning is essential to my point.

JUDGE: Overruled. Proceed.

ME: I quote from another TV script. In *The Case of the Fractured Fireman*, Mason is speaking to Drake. He says: "Found out anything about the missing ruby, yet, Paul?" and Drake replies: "Not yet, Perry." Mason says: "How many men have you got on it?" and Drake answers: "Johnstone, Everson, Charlesworth, and Goldberg. All good men." Whereupon Mason answers: "Better put two more men on it, Paul. We've got to have the answer by trial time."

Now I put it to you, Mason, that those men each receives one hundred dollars a day and expenses. At least that's what Sabre of London gets. Would you mind telling the court the total amount of the fee you received for this case?

MASON (*in a low voice*): There was no fee; this poor fireman had no money.

ME: Exactly! None of your clients have money because they are all innocent. Right.

MASON: Right.

ME: And innocent people never have any money—it's always been stolen from them. Right?

MASON: Right.

ME: Only crooks have money. Right?

MASON: Right.

ME: And you don't defend crooks?

MASON: No.

ME: Then where do you get the money to keep an enormous detective agency at your beck and call twenty-four hours a day?

MASON: I—I . . .

JUDGE: Witness must answer.

ME: Is it not a fact that after three solid years of work you now owe Paul Drake the sum of $457,892.37?

MASON: I—yes.

ME: And therefore, it would have been in your interest to have Paul Drake rubbed out?

HAMILTON BURGER (*rising*): Objection, your honour! The question is incompetent, irrelevant and immaterial.

JUDGE: Sustained.

ME (*smugly*): Withdraw the question. Now Mr. Mason, let us turn to another puzzling phase of your operations. I refer to the situation with Della Street!

MASON (*rising and half blind with rage*): I'll have you know that Miss Street is a fine, upstanding, clean-living American girl.

ME (*silkily*): No doubt, Mr. Mason. But it seems to me that her work is often beyond the call of duty.

MASON: Why, you—!

ME: By that I mean she works more than the 37½-hour week laid down by the International Union of Office Employees. She is there, in fact, from morning until night. In *The Case of the Parboiled Paperhanger*, for instance, your office was called at 10:30 p.m. and she answered the phone. She often installs your clients in motel rooms late at night (*The Case of the Cultured Corn Husker*) or in the wee small hours of the morning. And she appears, I might add, to have no social life of her own. Do you pay her overtime, Mason?

MASON: But, you see—

ME: Your Honour, will you instruct the witness to answer the question? Yes or no?

JUDGE: Witness will answer.

MASON: No!

ME: So she is more than a secretary to you? More than just an—employee?

MASON: She's—

ME: Is she or isn't she? Answer the question.

MASON: Yes.

ME: Are you in love with Della Street, Mr. Mason?

MASON (*goes white—goes red—then blurts it out*): Yes! Yes! Madly! Insatiably!

ME: But you were insanely jealous of Paul Drake, weren't you?

MASON: What do you mean?

ME: He was always hanging around the office, paying Miss Street little compliments . . . taking her out to dinner ostensibly at your request, because you were busy . . . calling her "beautiful" in front of you . . . chucking her under the chin. And you couldn't do anything about it, could you, Mason, because you owed Paul Drake $457,892.37 plus accumulated interest.

MASON: This is ridiculous!

ME: Not so ridiculous, Mason, when one considers that Drake, not you, owned every stick of furniture in that office. You had to let him have it in lieu of payment, as this document shows. Not only that, but *Drake wanted Della Street along with the furniture*. You were in his power, you were losing your girl, and there was only one way out: *murder!*

MASON (*buries face in hands*): Yes.

ME: You killed Paul Drake, Perry Mason! (*Lt. Tragg, who has had nothing to do until now, rises and clamps the handcuffs on Mason.*)

ME: Your Honour, the defence rests!

I walk out of the courtroom with my client, Della Street.

I Dreamed I Was
Superman In My
Maidenform Undershirt

I had a curious dream the other night, which recurs from time to time. I dreamed that I was a reporter on the Toronto *Daily Planet* and my name was Clark Kent. Well, that wasn't *really* my name; actually, my name was Superman. I came from the planet Krypton, see, and I had super-vision, super-strength, super-everything. Instead of underwear, I wore a natty Superman suit in blue and scarlet under my normal threads. I was dedicated to fighting crime in the Big City.

Whenever I heard of a mastermind controlling the underworld I would tear off my clothes in an alley or a phone booth and dash off into the sky crying "This is a job for Superman!" But if you read the comic books you know all about this anyway.

Well, in this dream it was a busy Tuesday morning on the *Daily Planet*. In my role as Clark Kent I had just turned in a three-paragraph story dealing with flower arrangement classes at the museum. My next assignment was the upcoming TTC meeting to decide on the new chairman of the transportation commission. I had my hat and overcoat on when my eye happened to catch the duplicate copy of an item turned in by my beautiful colleague, Lois Lane of the women's department. The story read as follows:

A master criminal of incredible cunning and avarice appears to be the Mr. Big behind the bootlegging of

thousands of pounds of coloured "spread" into local grocery stores, police said today.

It is believed that all of gangland is held in thralldom to this fiend incarnate whose infiltration of the butter market here is said to be one of the most callous criminal acts in history.

Thousands and thousands of farmers, unable to sell their butter, are destitute as the result of the machinations of this monster whose product, tinted a deceptive yellow, is selling for as little as fifty-two cents a pound.

It is believed that the gangland king has thousands of housewives in his employ colouring by hand pound after pound of brand-name margarine, which is then repackaged and bootlegged to the trade.

Police admit they are baffled in this case.

"It will take superhuman powers to bring this devil to justice," Inspector J. Harvey Grebe told the *Daily Planet.*

Fortunately, there is a private alley behind the *Daily Planet*, used mainly by delivery trucks. I slipped down at once, removing my overcoat, scarf and hat and piling them in an obscure corner. Then I took off my newly tailored three-piece Ivy League suit, folded it neatly and placed it on top of the overcoat. I removed shirt, tie, tie clip, cufflinks, socks and shoes and laid them in the alley, too. Then, costumed as the Man of Steel, I headed for Roncesvalles and a small grocery store with a mighty bound. It was here that my super-senses told me I would find the key to the riddle.

The trouble was I kept worrying about my suit back there

in the alley. It had started to rain and I wondered how I would look covering the TTC all rumpled and muddy.

The TTC! I had forgotten my assignment, and the deadline for the Three Star Edition was only minutes away! I bounded back into the alley, leaped into my sodden clothes, assumed the role of Clark Kent and took the subway to Davisville, just in time. I phoned the story in to rewrite and then searched about for some place to change my clothes again so I could reassume my role of Superman.

First, I went down to the Bi-Way and bought some of those folding coat hangers that travellers find so useful; also a clothes brush and whisk. I then searched about for an obscure telephone booth since I recalled, in my dream, that Superman in the comic books was always removing his clothing in obscure telephone booths when he was not using unfrequented alleyways.

I first stepped into one of the phone booths in the Park Plaza Hotel, but this proved impossible. A lineup of people formed, and one of them began hammering on the door, so I got out of there and headed for Exhibition Park; the phones there do not work except at Exhibition time. I carefully removed my outer clothing and hung it neatly on the coat hangers. I was glad to get out of it since my Superman suit had got damp in the rain, and I was starting to itch.

Then in another mighty bound I headed back to the innocent-looking grocery store on Roncesvalles.

I took up a position on the roof and waited for one of the mastermind's spies to make an appearance with the illegally coloured margarine. Unfortunately, I could not wait too long because at 2 p.m. I had to interview a man who was roller skating around the world. I left my post shortly before the hour to retrieve my clothes in the telephone booth, but somebody had stolen them, so I was forced to go home and get a new suit. I was beginning to see the problems facing Superman. Fortunately, I had twenty-seven new suits hanging in my closet for just such an emergency. I figure Superman goes through about three a day.

I interviewed the champion roller skater, wrote the story and turned it in to the city desk. I had scarcely finished when Lois Lane burst into the women's department crying that the margarine fiend had struck again!

There was no time for hesitation now. Our own alleyway was jammed with delivery trucks loading Final Editions, every phone booth was in use, and so in desperation I decided to use Pearl Street, a one-way alley directly north of King Street. I was just pulling off my trousers, trying to avoid creasing them, when a society columnist for the *Globe and Mail*, slipping out the back way for a spot of sherry, uttered a piercing shriek. Several policemen arrived, and I was taken off and charged with indecent exposure in a public place. Oh, the shame of it!

Unfortunately, my own newspaper would offer me little protection in court, since I had scarcely been seen around the office for days. One of the Crown witnesses at the ensuing trial—a newspaper delivery driver—testified that on several occasions he had seen me removing my clothing in the alley behind the *Daily Planet*. I was taken off to prison where, as luck would have it, my cellmate was the Margarine

Fiend, who was apprehended the same day as a result of clever police work by Toronto's finest.

And that is the end of my dream, which, incidentally, was in wide screen and colour. Wonder what's showing tonight?

Down With Those
Foreign TV Stars!

. . . Some critics have complained that the Canadian Opera Company has been favouring foreign stars in its current productions when it ought to be concentrating on our Canadian talent.
                                                    —News Item

• • • • • •

MET USING ITALIAN STARS TO SING FOREIGN OPERAS—CRITIC

Strong criticism was voiced today by New York critics over the Metropolitan Opera Company's invidious practice of employing non-American talent in many of the leading roles in its major operas.

"Why can't these parts be given to deserving U.S. singers?" queried Rathscallen Void, supporter of a distinctive American way of life, in his copyright column published today.

Void wrote that he was shocked to discover that Lauritz Melchior, a Danish nationalist and smorgasbord enthusiast, had apparently sung many leading Wagnerian roles at the Met and also that other foreign "imports," notably Kirsten Flagstad, Maria Callas, and Teresa Stratas, had been given fat contracts from time to time, thus squeezing out deserving New York divas.

The practice of attracting glamorous foreign names had been begun, he said, by Edward Johnson, a Canadian, who did not understand U.S. ways, and continued by Rudolf Bing, who, he charged, had used many Italian operas by Verdi,

Puccini and others in preference to operas written by worthy American writers and composers.

"Worse than this," Void wrote, "these operas have actually starred Italian performers, singing in their language. How can we establish a distinctive national culture when our greatest cultural centre turns its back on America and imports foreign stars, foreign writers, foreign musicians and even foreign conductors, such as the late Toscanini, to the detriment of our own artists?"

Void's revelations caused an immediate sensation and may force a congressional investigation into the use of foreigners in a publicly supported cultural centre.

• • • • • •

CLAIMS N.Y. RANGERS SWAMPED
WITH DISGUISED CANUCK IMPORTS

An all-out attack on the New York Rangers was launched today after a speaker at the annual conference of the All-American Sportswriters of America revealed that the famous hockey team had been in the habit of using foreign "imports."

Gerard Dunnell, dean of American sportswriters and himself a U.S.-born hockey player (for the short-lived Dartmouth Comets), stunned the annual dinner meeting with his revelations.

Dunnell stated categorically that many players on the Rangers were actually Canadians disguised as Americans and went on to charge that the Detroit Red Wings, Chicago Black Hawks, and Boston Bruins were also using imports in an attempt to "glamorize the sport" to the detriment of home-grown players.

The cunning foreigners were able to infiltrate the American teams, he said, because they "looked, acted, thought, talked and played like Americans."

"They have even adopted typically American names like Vasco, Babando and Nesterenko," he told his stunned listeners.

The practice of loading American teams with imports—and without any apparent quota system to keep the matter in check—was endangering American sovereignty, Dunnell stated.

"Americans have been placed in the unenviable position of being hewers of wood and drawers of water to Canadian hockey moguls," he declared, adding that if the situation continues, the United States will soon be little more than an outpost of Canada.

• • • • • •

CHARGE U.S. NETWORKS PREFER
TORONTO GLAMOUR TO U.S. TALENT

Harsh words for all three U.S. radio and television networks for their neglect of homegrown talent were voiced today at the annual Conference of the Arts held in Bathrobe, Wisconsin.

Speaker after speaker denounced U.S. television in particular for promoting glamorous foreign stars in preference to their native counterparts.

Time and again, it was claimed, U.S. producers sought out expensive performers from other countries—such as Christopher Plummer, Céline Dion, John Cleese, and Alan Thicke—when their roles could easily have been filled by struggling U.S. hopefuls.

The conference was especially critical of the practice of

importing Canadian actors and directors to U.S. television simply because the "name power" of the Canadians made them appear more glamorous to U.S. audiences. These Canadians were often paid huge fees, it was charged, while Americans had to be content with union-scale payments.

One speaker charged that the problem was not a new one. Historically, he said, Canadian stars have always dominated Hollywood productions. The use of a Canadian cowhand, Lorne Greene, in an adult western series was particularly enraging. So was the employment of a well-known Canadian medical man, Raymond Massey, in a TV series about a young doctor. At the time a brief was sent to the American Medical Association urging that a Harvard man be used as a replacement or "stand by," but nothing came of it.

The continual use of Canadian Mounties in many filmed series drew a storm of criticism from the floor. "Surely this great country is not so bereft of heroes of its own that we must choose myth-figures from the Canadian past to bolster our native adventure tales!" cried one delegate.

The blanket importing of dozens of actors from the Stratford Shakespearean Festival drew the wrath of the conference president, Arundel Sneath, who pointed out that at least six Canadians would be used in a forthcoming Hallmark production of *Cyrano de Bergerac*.

Mr. Sneath made it clear that he was not attacking Canadian culture. "There is nothing wrong with Canadian culture," he said, "but the point is that it is, after all, distinctively Canadian. Must we Americans adopt it holus-bolus simply because it has a certain foreign glamour? Surely we can produce something distinctive of our own without blindly reaching across the border to accept Canadian values, Canadian money and Canadian cultural patterns."

Several performers added to the discussion by announcing that they had received so much discouragement in their own country that they were thinking of leaving for Toronto "where Americans are really appreciated."

I'm Cryin', Yes,
I'm Cryin' For Those
Happy Songs of Yore

Remember the hurtin' songs of the mid-century? Probably not; they were hardly memorable. It is true that, unlike more modern works, you could actually understand the lyrics; but that's not much of an accolade. It was an odd period, when grown men could be heard sobbing their hearts out and the disc jockeys were up to their ankles in teardrops.

In 1951, an emaciated crooner named Johnnie Ray had two huge hits on the charts—both about crying. One was called simply "Cry" and the other "The Little White Cloud That Cried." Ray's specialty was that he could cry on cue and in tune. I do not recall any of his appearances—and there were many—in which he wasn't sobbing his heart out. If your sweetheart sends a letter of goodbye, he told us, as the tears trickled down his cheeks, then you'll know that you'll feel better if you cry. Our century has much to answer for, but Johnnie-baby is right near the top of the big list along with the Grand Kleagle and Alan the Eagle.

The tears I cry for you could fill an ocean
But you don't know how many years I cry . . .

Remember that one? It was introduced by an announcer who burbled into the microphone that it was "Another Hurtin' Song from CHOO," thereby making it clear that there was more than one. Until that moment—it was the fall of

'58—I had thought it was the *same* song, but I was dead wrong. There were fourteen current hits that season all about cryin', weepin', and teardrops.

> **Whoops, there goes a teardrop**
> **Rolling down my face,**
> **If you cry when you're in love**
> **It sure ain't no disgrace . . .**

When I was growing up, we did not have such songs; but then times were terrible and there were other things to cry about. The songs of the thirties were almost all gay—full of wonder, joy, and optimism. Girls were not crushed by oncoming trains, nor did boys die in flaming sports cars as they did in the later teen hits. Margo did not hit the dirt in a sickening way to leave Jim alone on his wedding day; there were no Teen Angels or Artificial Flowers. We, each of us, had a Pocketful of Dreams, the Night Was Filled with Music, we Whistled While We Worked, and Who Was Afraid of the Big, Bad Wolf? Only when prosperity stopped lurking around the corner and boom times returned did we begin to cry uncontrollably.

In the old hungry years we kept that old stiff upper lip even when our girl left us. Dinner for One, Please James, we told the butler, adding that, though madame would not be dining, he might as well bring the wine in. With a real butler and a jug of wine, who needed a girl anyway?

> *There's a broken heart for ev'ry song on the jukebox*
> *Someone's teardrops fall for ev'ry tune it plays . . .*

Broken hearts were few and far between in the hits of the Depression. The songs were full of wishful thinking about butlers and faraway places. "It" happened in Old Monterey and also on the Isle of Capri, in Blue Hawaii and Down Mexico Way. We sailed away to Treasure Island or the beach at Bali-Bali, and we sang of the West Wind (blowing over land and sea) or the Trade Winds or the Moon over Miami or Paris in the Spring. Love lay just Beyond the Blue Horizon.

> ***The bitter earth***
> > ***What fruit it shares***
> ***What good is love***
> > ***When no one cares?***

The songwriters of the thirties had their eyes, not on the earth, but on the stars. They sang of Heaven and the Moon (which Got in Our Eyes); and when you Wished on the Moon, it all came true. Love in those days was almost always requited. The Blue Moon turned, in the final chorus, to gold, and We Told Every Little Star all about it. Wonder of wonders! If the Moon Turned Green and rivers began to roll upstream and this was all a crazy dream we couldn't be more surprised. But then dreams were our business. A girl was a Dream Walking—heaven in our arms. You Couldn't Stop Us from Dreaming and sometimes we Dreamed Too Much. With Our Eyes Wide Open, We Were Dreaming, and When We Grew Too Old to Dream We'd Still Have You to Remember.

Midnight, oh what a lonely time to weep, I oughta know
Midnight, I should have been fast asleep, hours ago
Still I'm cryin, I'm cryin', 'cause I miss you so . . .

"If they have gold statuettes for tears and regrets, I'd be a legend in my time," one man sobbed. There were few regrets in the songs of the thirties. It is true that one hit, "Brother, Can You Spare a Dime?" mirrored the times perfectly and evokes them today; but this song was a notable exception. "C'mon, Get Happy!" the crooners carolled; "Smile, Darn Ya, Smile!" We didn't own overcoats but We Had Our Love to Keep Us Warm. It was always a Lovely Day to be Caught in the Rain. And every time it did, it rained Pennies from Heaven. We walked down the Sunny Side of the Street with Our Hat on the Side of Our Head, and it was forever June in January. Worries? Forget 'em! *Let's Have Another Cup of Coffee and Let's Have Another Piece of Pie . . . We'll Make Hay While the Sun Shines . . . Isn't Love the Grandest Thing?*

I'm sorry, so sorry that I was such a fool
I didn't know love could be so cruel . . .

"Sorry" was the operative word in the hits of the fifties and sixties, but in my day the big word was "sweet." The adjective has been virtually banned from the airwaves. But I can remember when Love Was the Sweetest Thing; when girls were Sweet and Lovely, sweeter than the flowers in May; when Sweet Was the Word For You. We didn't say

Baby, Be My Queen of Hearts, we said Stay As Sweet As
You Are, and even if a girl was a bit of a headache, she was
A Sweet Little Headache.

> *It's over and done with*
> *The date has been set*
> *There's no time for talking*
> *Too late for regret*
> *Yes, all I can say is congratulations.*
> *Congratulations for breaking my heart.*

I suspect our attitude toward women, in our songs anyway, was a little more tolerant later because we had faith
in the Object of Our Affections: she could go where she
wanted to go, do what she wanted to do, and we didn't care
because we trusted her. There is a lack of cheerful security
in the later songs. I Know You'll Be Tempted to Stray While
I'm Away, sobbed the songwriter. But, Baby, Wait! Wait!
Wait! Somehow one gets the idea she ain't agonna wait.
There was a kind of hopelessness in the songs that came later.
Is There Any Chance You and I Could Start All Over? one
asked. (None.) Only the Lonely Know Why I Cry wept a second. There was one note of optimism, however, in a third:
*"It doesn't hurt so much to hear your name. I think I'll make
it. I'm getting better."*

This is a long way removed from "Here's To Romance!"
or "Let My Song Fill Your Heart" or "Wake Up and Live" or
"Cheerful Little Earful."

I am reminded, somehow, of the songs my mother used

to sing—songs from the last century with titles like "Softly She Turned from the Grave and Cried," or "He Laid a Wreath of Roses on Her Cold and Chilly Brow." A century later our lyrics had come full circle and we were back where we began when Tin Pan Alley was a lane.

> *Miss Molly fell ill and the sweet angels took her,*
> *Young Timmy, he died of regret.*
> *The willow was sad and the willow bowed down*
> *And the willow is weeping yet.*

Eight

THE FINAL ABSURDITY

Why Not a Song About Toronto to Mark the Millennium?

It is sad that when one arrives at Toronto by plane, car or rail, no sudden melody, no familiar lyrics spring to mind as in other leading cities.

One thinks of such tunes as "San Francisco," "Chicago," "New York, New York (It's a Wonderful Town)," "Meet Me in St. Louis," "April in Paris," and even "Saskatoon, Saskatchewan." Yet nothing comparable has been written about Toronto.

With the Millennium fast approaching, I have tried in some measure to fill this gap, but I'm not certain I've been too successful. However, rather than write just one Toronto song, I've written several variations, for I discover that songs about cities fall into various categories.

There is, for example, the exultant paean-of-praise:

Toronto! Toronto!
It's a wonderful city!
It may not be handsome,
It may not be pretty,
It may not be friendly,
It may not be sportive
In fact it may be
That it's rather abortive;
It may make you cry
And it may make you curse;
But if you've GOT to live here
You could maybe do worse.

That's somehow not quite right, I fear. Perhaps a bit of the nostalgic "hometown" sort of thing would be more fitting:

I am walking down old Yonge Street and I'm dreaming,
I'm dreaming of the town that I adore;
Now to you it may seem old and sort of shabby
But to me it is a place I can't abhor.
I am turning east on Richmond and I'm thinking
Of those moonlight nights on which we used to spoon,
And as I reach Victoria, I keep pining—
I keep pining for my hometown: Saskatoon.

Is it possible that the far-away-from-home theme would be preferable?

Oh, it's Saturday night on Dundas
And it's there I long to be—
From Parliament to Sherbourne
There's no other place for me.
At every tavern portal
They're spoiling for a fight:
How I long to hear those whistles
And those sirens in the night!
So, though I walk on foreign strands,
My memories aren't gone
As I dream of Sunday morning
In a cell beside the Don!

Yet somehow that kind of song just doesn't work when

applied to Toronto. The Bowery, yes; Toronto, no. What's wanted, I believe, is some romantic love lyric, tying the city up with some beautiful girl.

I met her in Toronto
When the snow was turning brown,
And whispered softly in her ear:
"Let's both get out of town!"

No, no, no! Let's start afresh, shall we?

When it's winter in Toronto,
I'm coming back to you.
Little sweetheart of Spadina
Your nose is turning blue.
Once again I say I love you,
As the wind begins to screech;
When it's winter in Toronto
I will meet you in Palm Beach.

I think what's wrong is that all this poetry, lyrical though it may be, lacks the strong feeling of romance and nostalgia that is evoked by the use of real place names and old, familiar rendezvous—like the Champs Élysées and the Café de Paris in those songs about Paris. One more try:

There's a girl from old Toronto
Who haunts my nightly slumber;
I met her in Etobicoke

Beside the burbling Humber.
She was born just east of Dufferin
And I sort of liked her looks,
So we went to all those places
You read about in books:
Oh, those mad, mad nights at Shopsy's!
Those days at Honest Ed's!
The CNE romances
Behind the cattle sheds!
And riding on the subway
Where anything can happen—
And those fascinating visits
To historic Scadding Cabin!
Those days at the Museum
Viewing busts of ancient rulers!
Those Sundays window shopping
At Peoples Credit Jewellers!

> *With that girl from old Toronto,*
> *That girl I used to know*
> *Until she up and married*
> *And moved to Buffalo.*

About the Author

Pierre Berton, Canada's favourite popular historian, was born in the Yukon and educated at UBC. He has received three Governor General's Awards for non-fiction, two Nellies for broadcasting, two National Newspaper Awards, the Stephen Leacock Medal for Humour, and the National History Society's first Award for "distinguished achievement in popularizing Canadian history." He holds eleven honorary degrees, is a member of the Newsman's Hall of Fame, and is a Companion of the Order of Canada. This is his forty-seventh book.